TABLE OF CONTENTS

- TELL THE TIME AND DRAW THE HANDS ON THE CLOCK **DAYS 13-20**

- MATCHING AND READING ANALOG & DIGITAL CLOCKS **DAYS 13-20**

- ADDING AND SUBTRACTING TIME **DAYS 13-20**

- ELAPSED TIME USING TWO CLOCKS **DAYS 13-20**

- ELAPSED TIME TABLES **DAYS 13-20**

- CONVERSION OF TIME UNITS **DAYS 13-20**

- ELAPSED DAYS, WEEKS, MONTHS, AND YEARS **DAYS 13-20**

ANSWER KEY IN BACK

Name: _____ Date: _____

PAGE 1

What Time Is It ?

Telling the Time Workbook
100 Practice pages

This Book Belongs To:

.................Scarlett..

By π Math

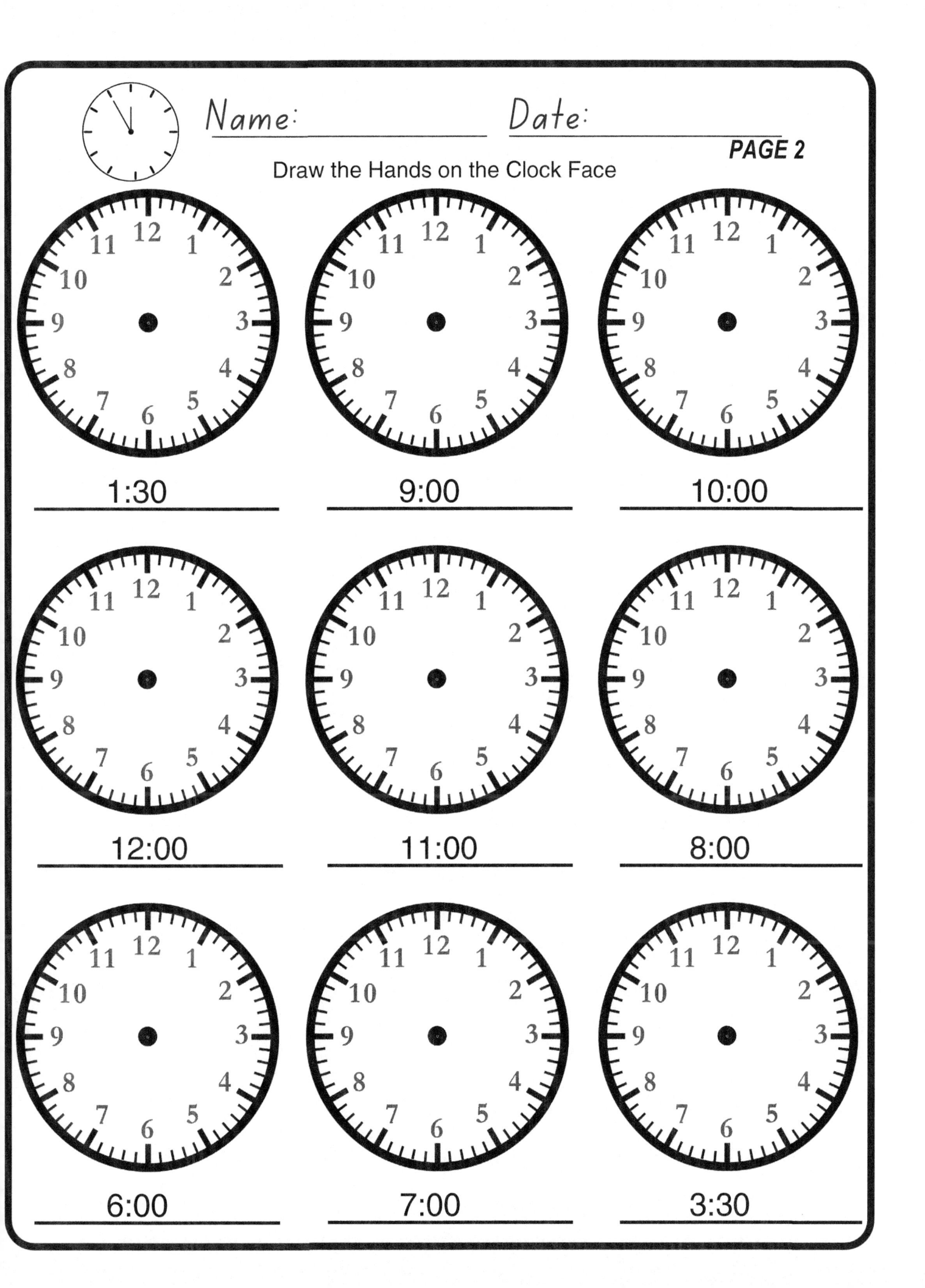

Name: _____ **Date:** _____

PAGE 2

Draw the Hands on the Clock Face

1:30	9:00	10:00
12:00	11:00	8:00
6:00	7:00	3:30

Name: _____   Date: _____

PAGE 3

What Time Is It ?

_____   _____   _____

_____   _____   _____

_____   _____   _____

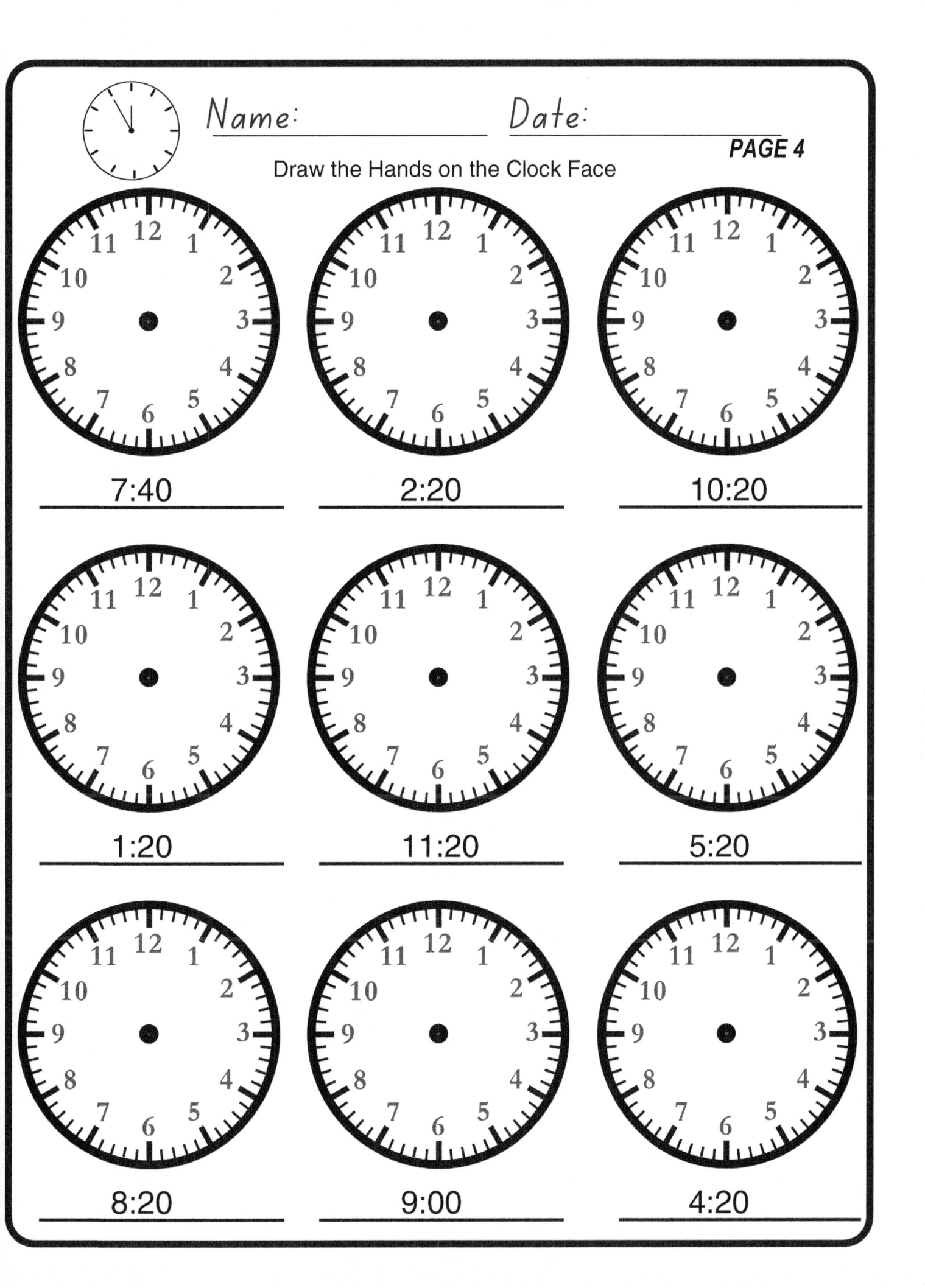

Name: _____   Date: _____

PAGE 4

Draw the Hands on the Clock Face

7:40   2:20   10:20

1:20   11:20   5:20

8:20   9:00   4:20

Name: _____ Date: _____

PAGE 5

What Time Is It ?

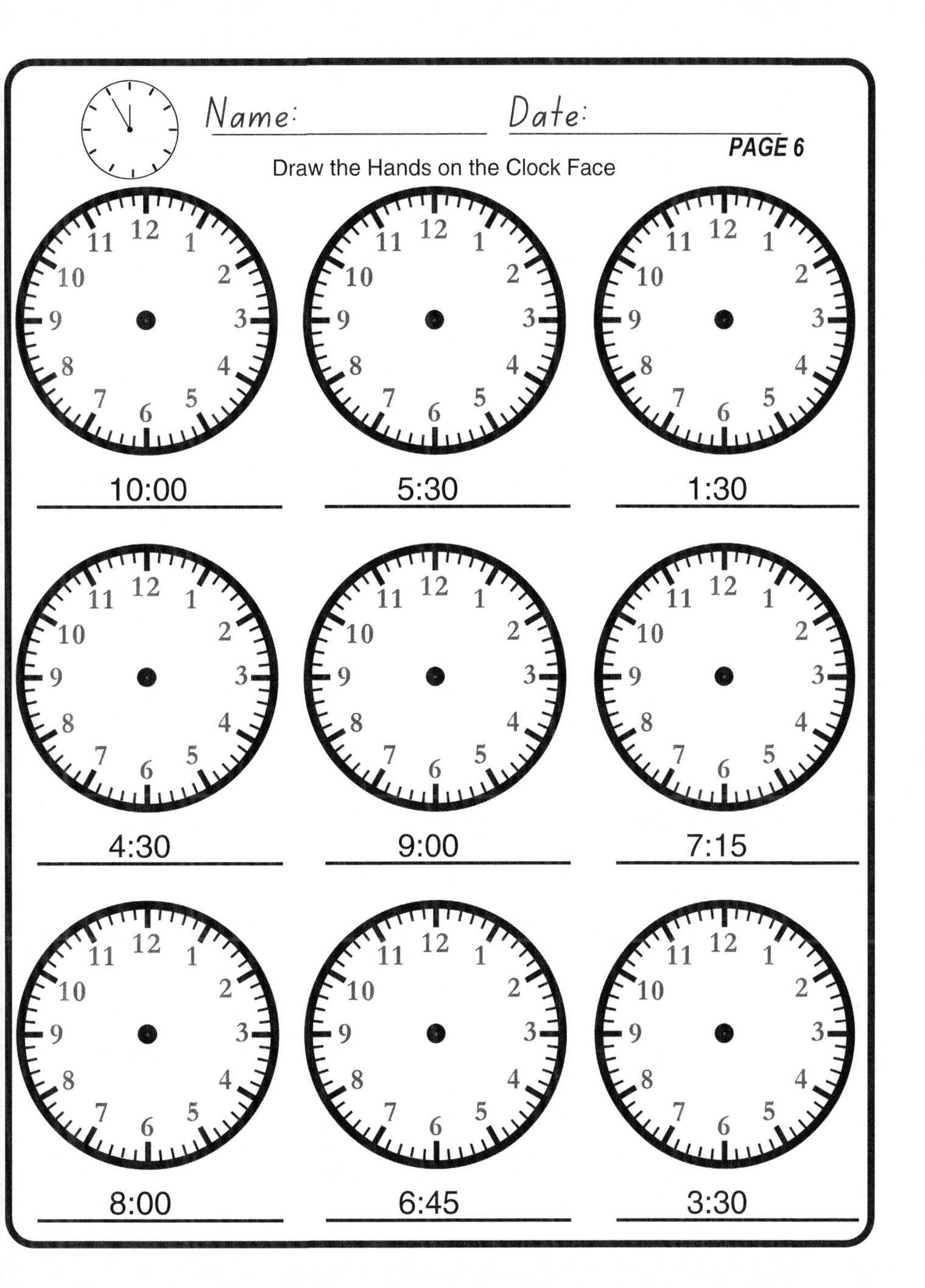

Name: _____ **Date:** _____

PAGE 6

Draw the Hands on the Clock Face

10:00	5:30	1:30
4:30	9:00	7:15
8:00	6:45	3:30

Name: _____ Date: _____

PAGE 7

What Time Is It ?

_____   _____   _____

_____   _____   _____

_____   _____   _____

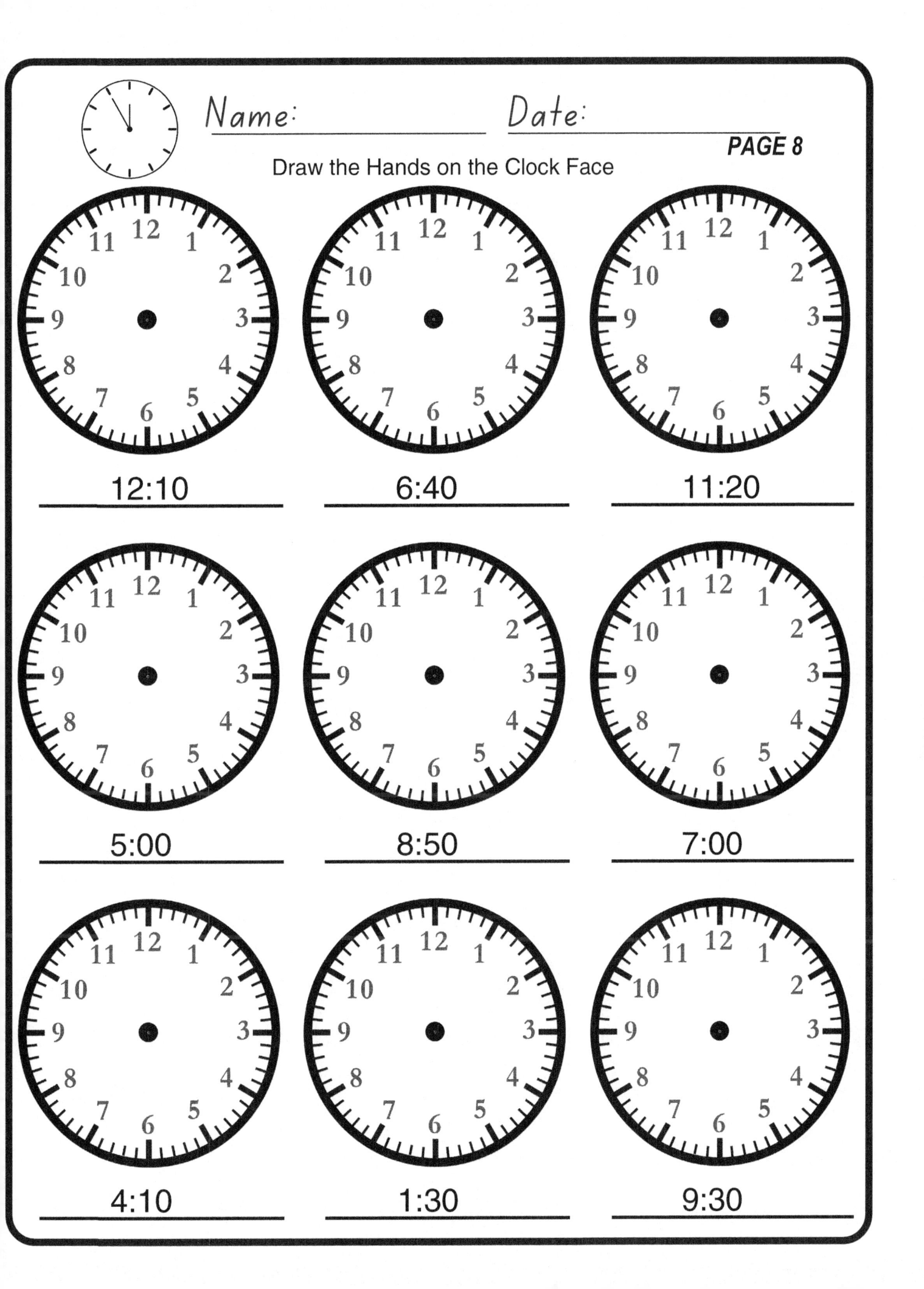

Name: _____ Date: _____

PAGE 8

Draw the Hands on the Clock Face

12:10	6:40	11:20
5:00	8:50	7:00
4:10	1:30	9:30

Name: _____ Date: _____

PAGE 9

What Time Is It ?

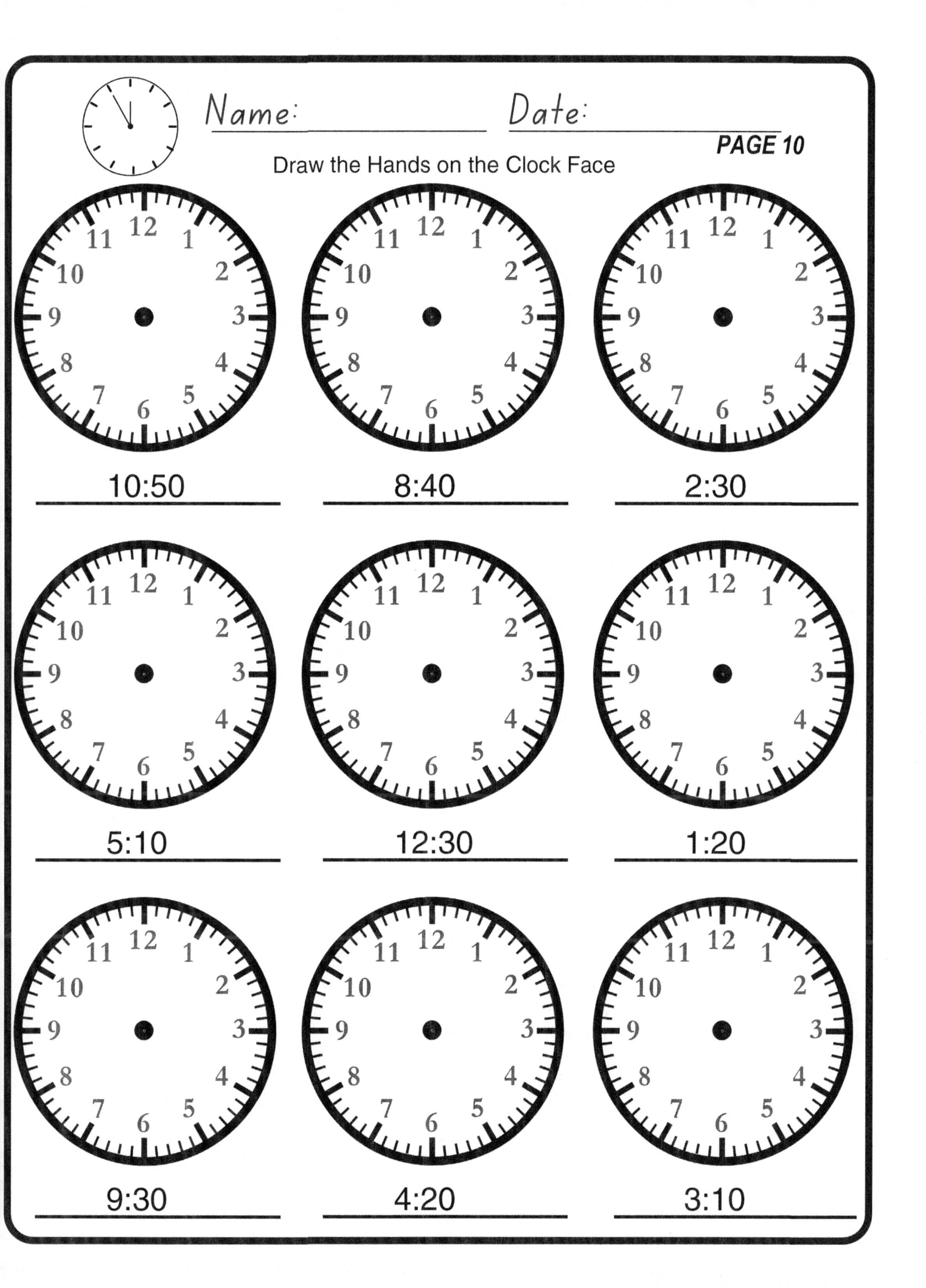

Name: _____ **Date:** _____

PAGE 10

Draw the Hands on the Clock Face

10:50

8:40

2:30

5:10

12:30

1:20

9:30

4:20

3:10

Name: _____ Date: _____

PAGE 11

What Time Is It ?

_____   _____   _____

_____   _____   _____

_____   _____   _____

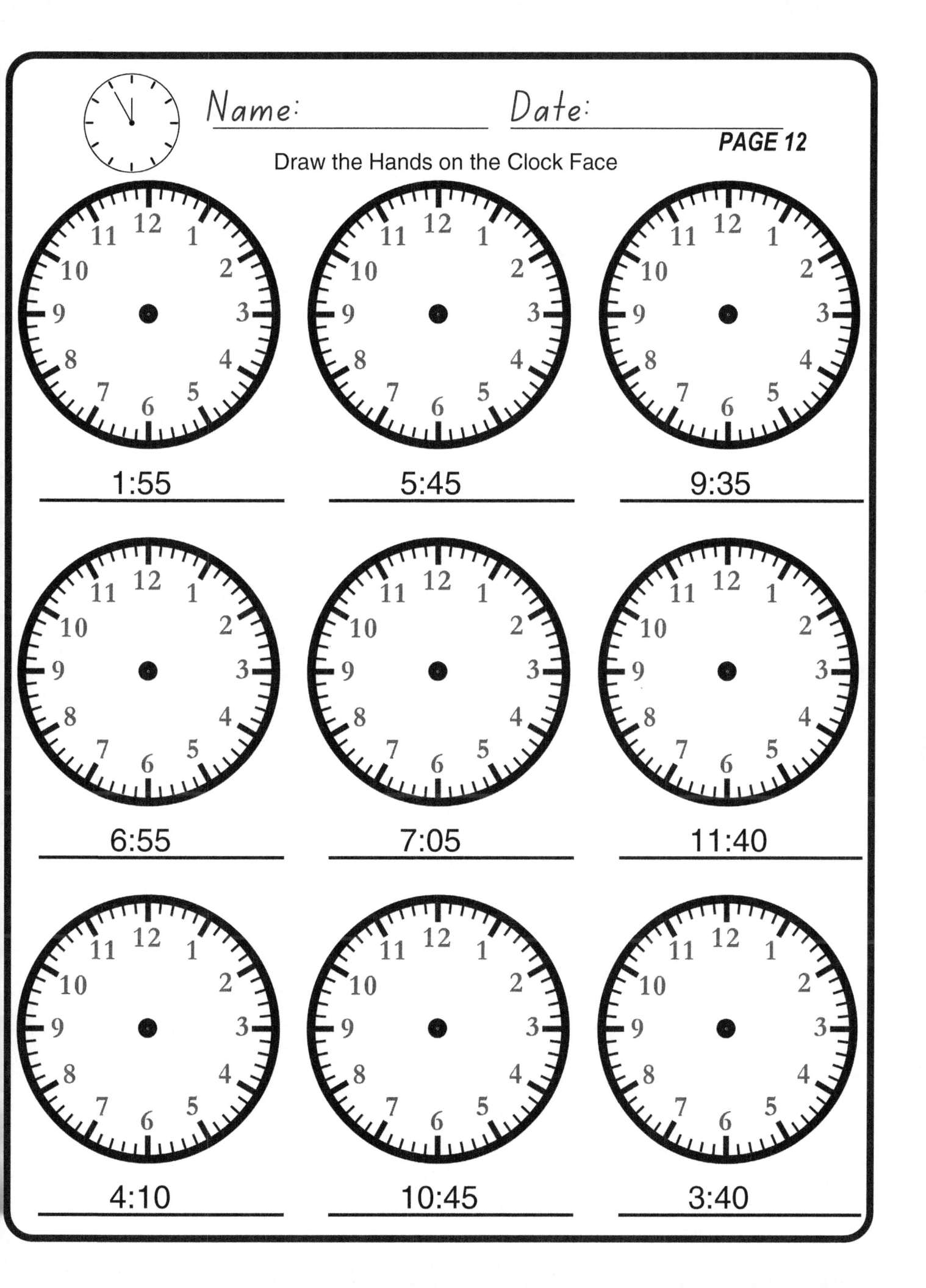

Name: _____ Date: _____

PAGE 12

Draw the Hands on the Clock Face

| 1:55 | 5:45 | 9:35 |

| 6:55 | 7:05 | 11:40 |

| 4:10 | 10:45 | 3:40 |

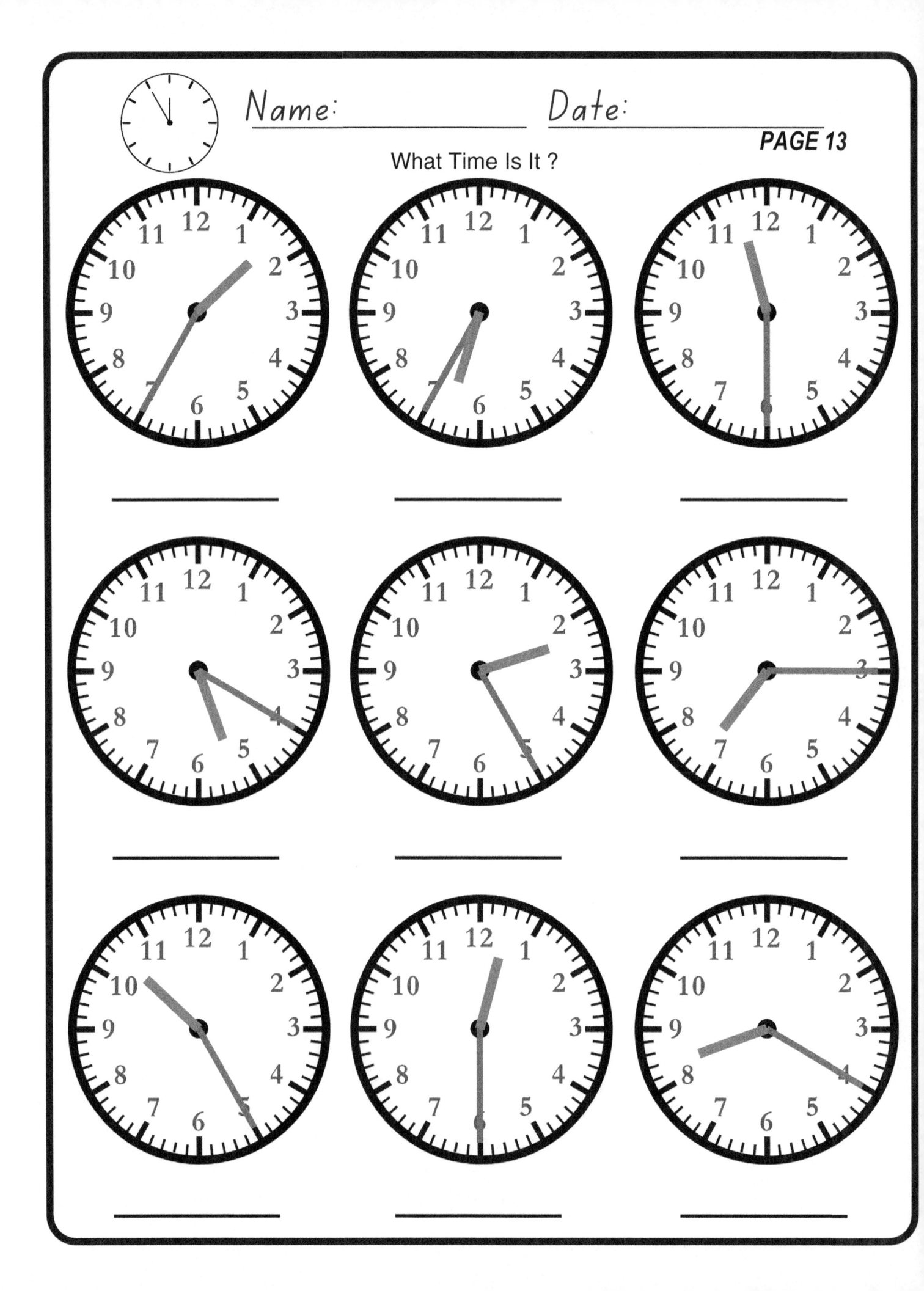

Name: _____ Date: _____

PAGE 13

What Time Is It ?

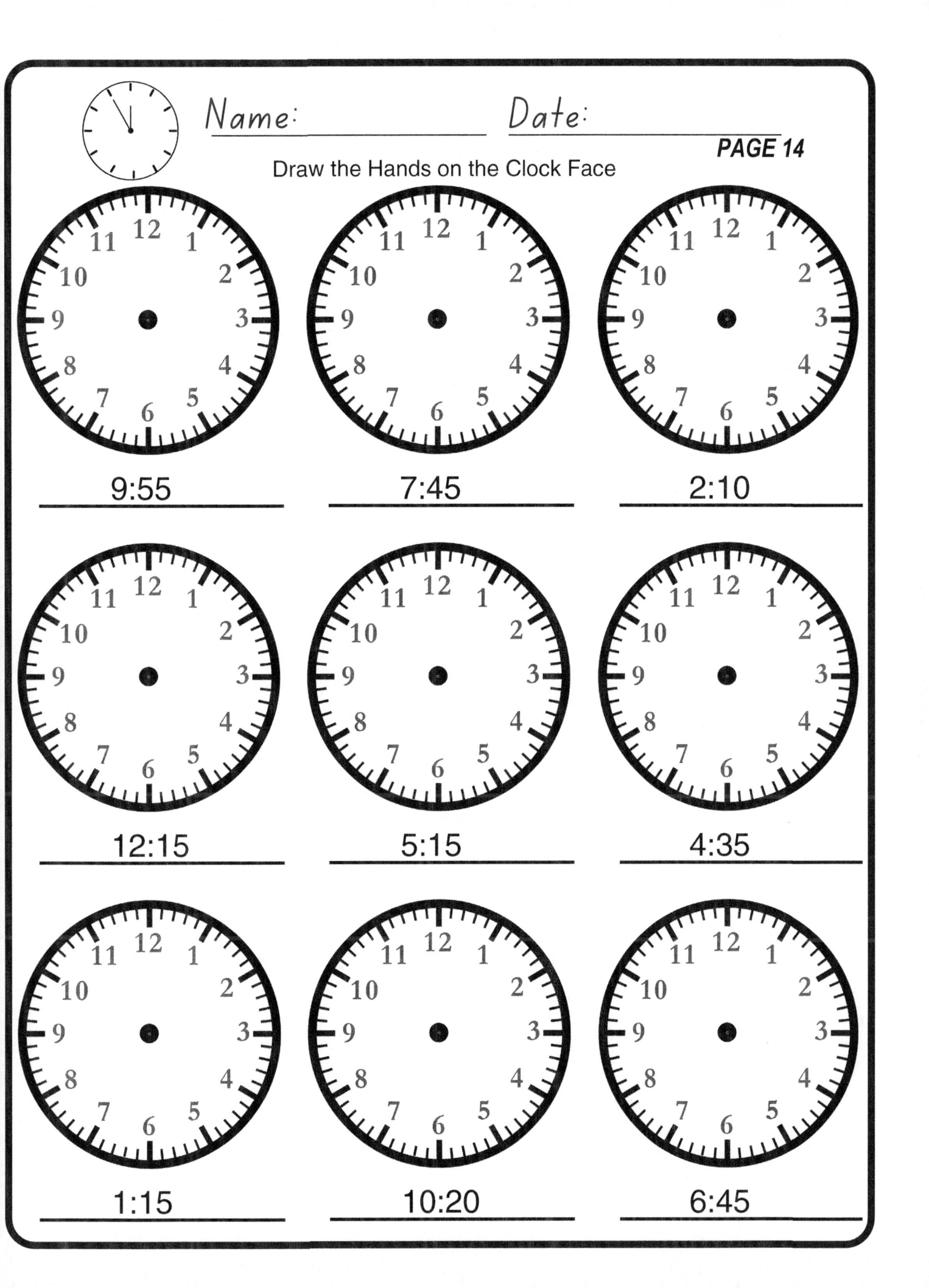

Name: _____ Date: _____

PAGE 14

Draw the Hands on the Clock Face

9:55

7:45

2:10

12:15

5:15

4:35

1:15

10:20

6:45

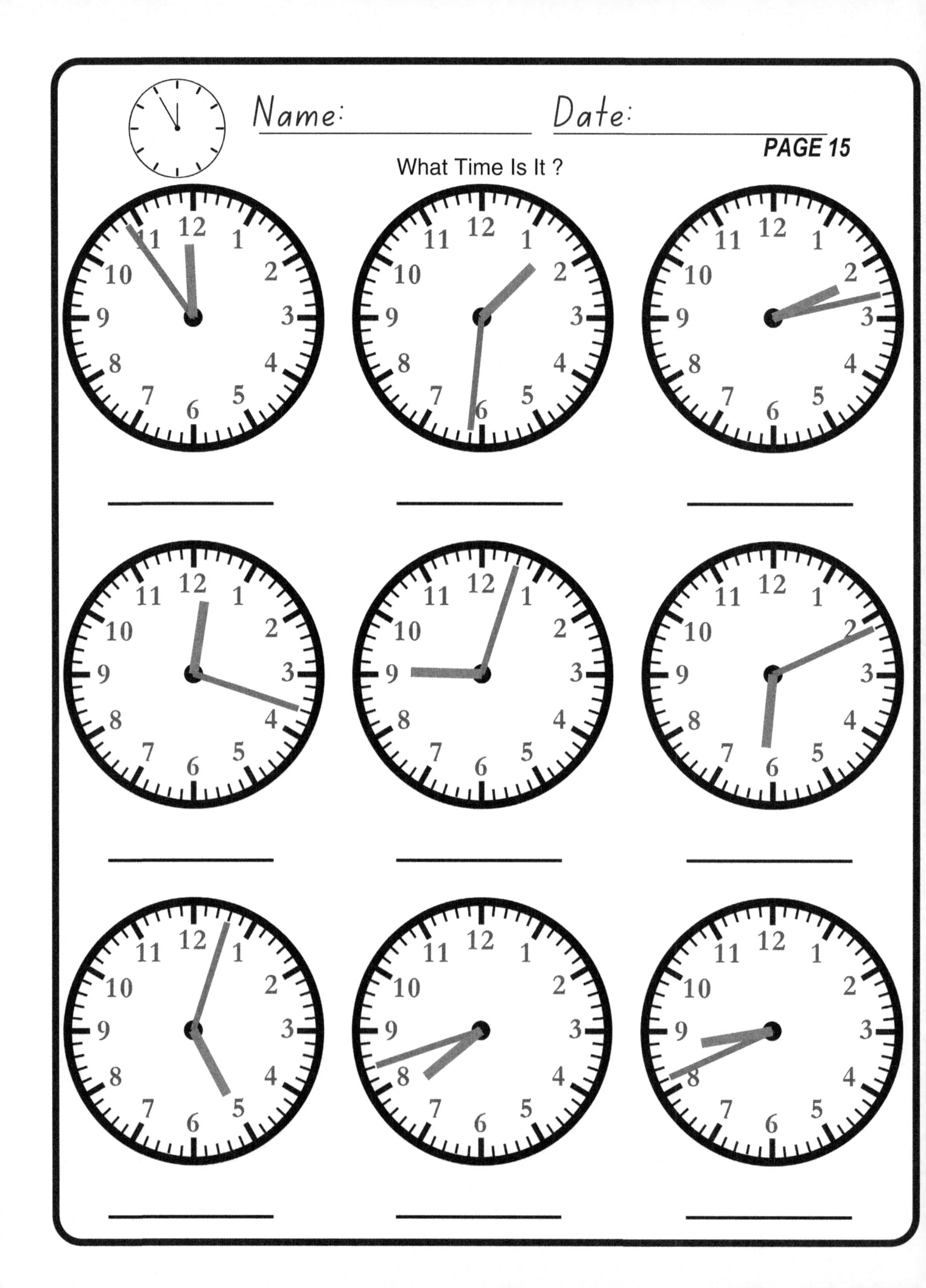

Name: _____ **Date:** _____

PAGE 15

What Time Is It ?

_____ _____ _____

_____ _____ _____

_____ _____ _____

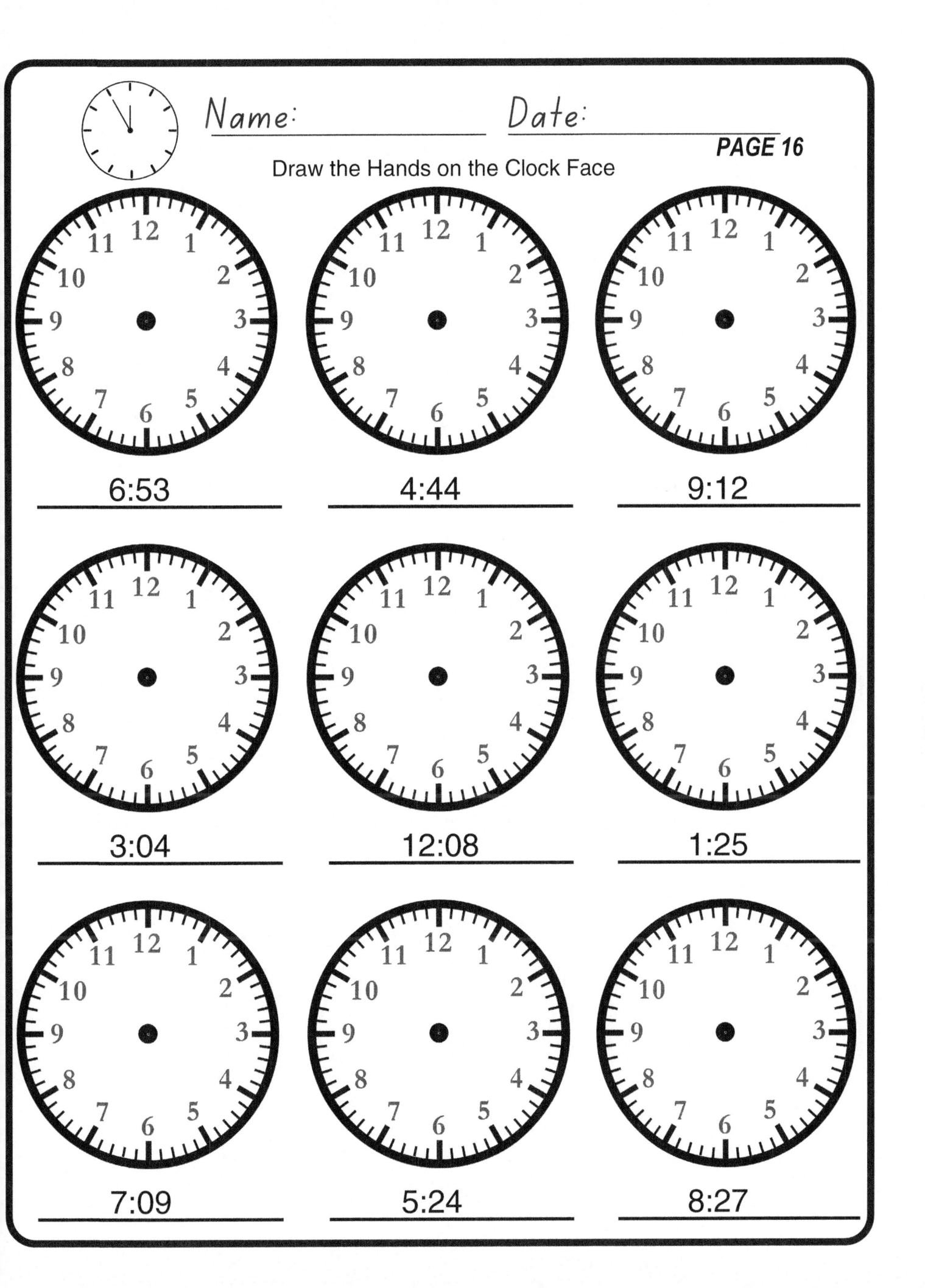

Name: _____ Date: _____

PAGE 16

Draw the Hands on the Clock Face

6:53   4:44   9:12

3:04   12:08   1:25

7:09   5:24   8:27

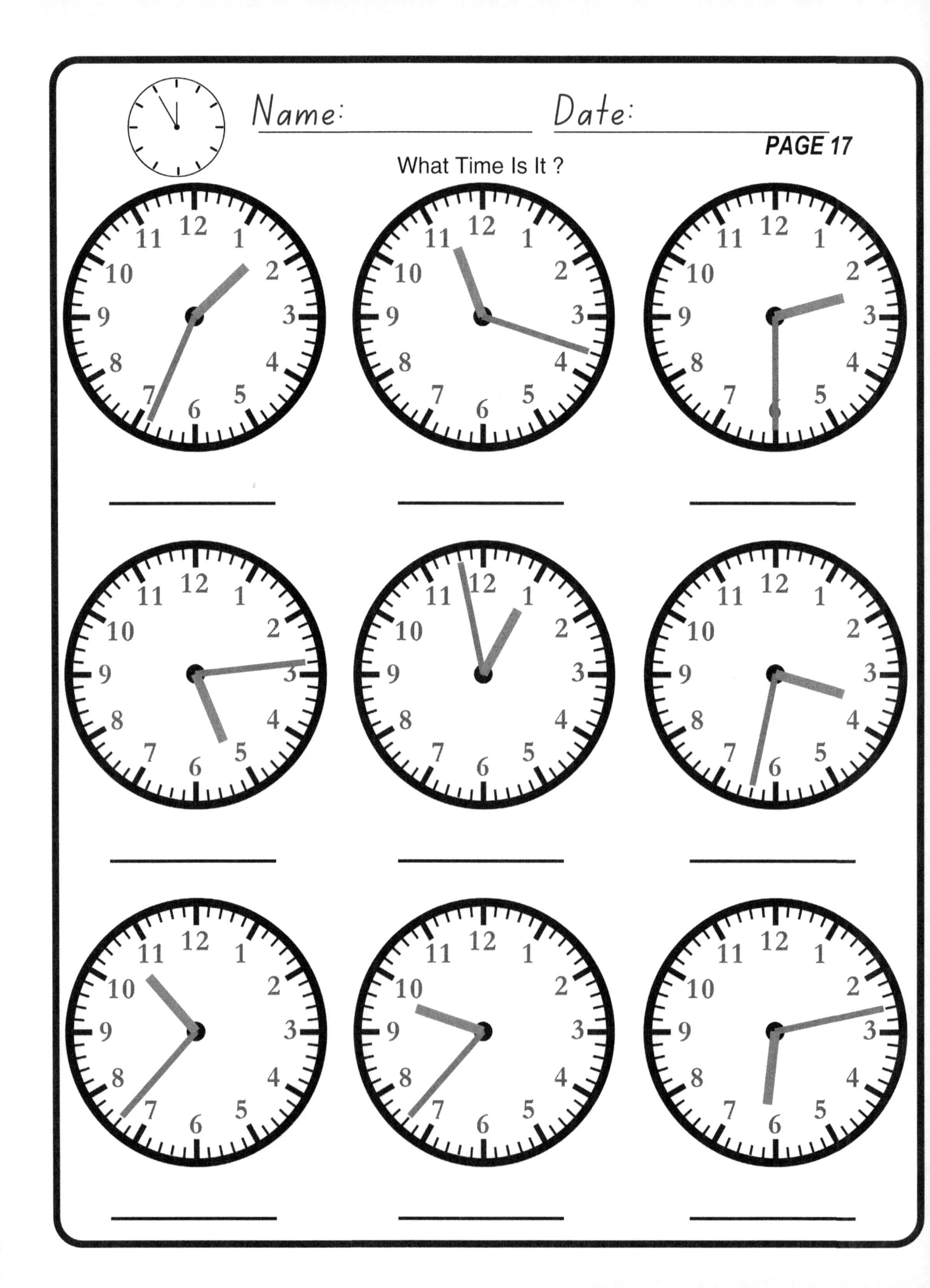

Name: Date:

PAGE 17

What Time Is It ?

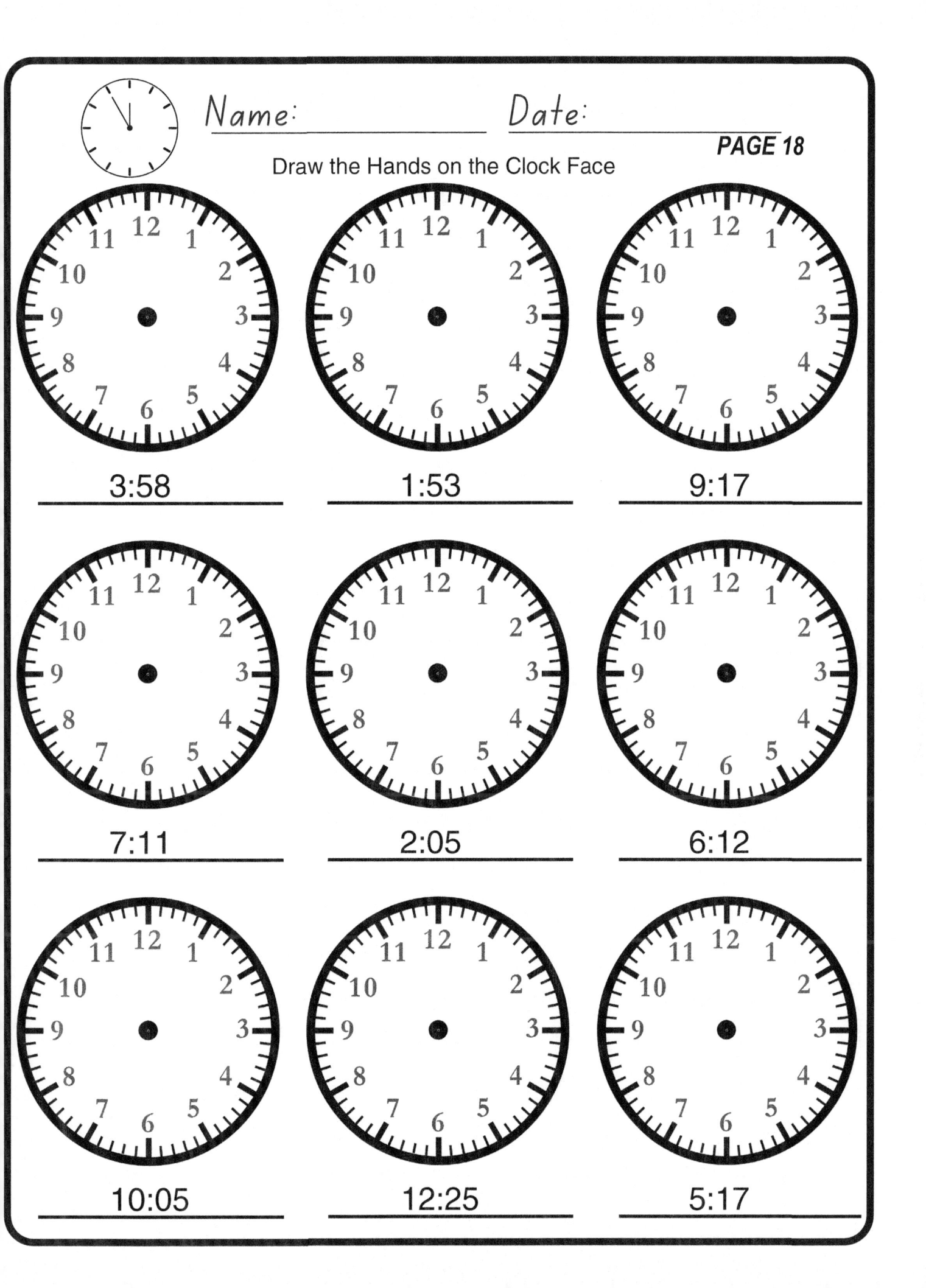

Name: _____ Date: _____

PAGE 18

Draw the Hands on the Clock Face

3:58

1:53

9:17

7:11

2:05

6:12

10:05

12:25

5:17

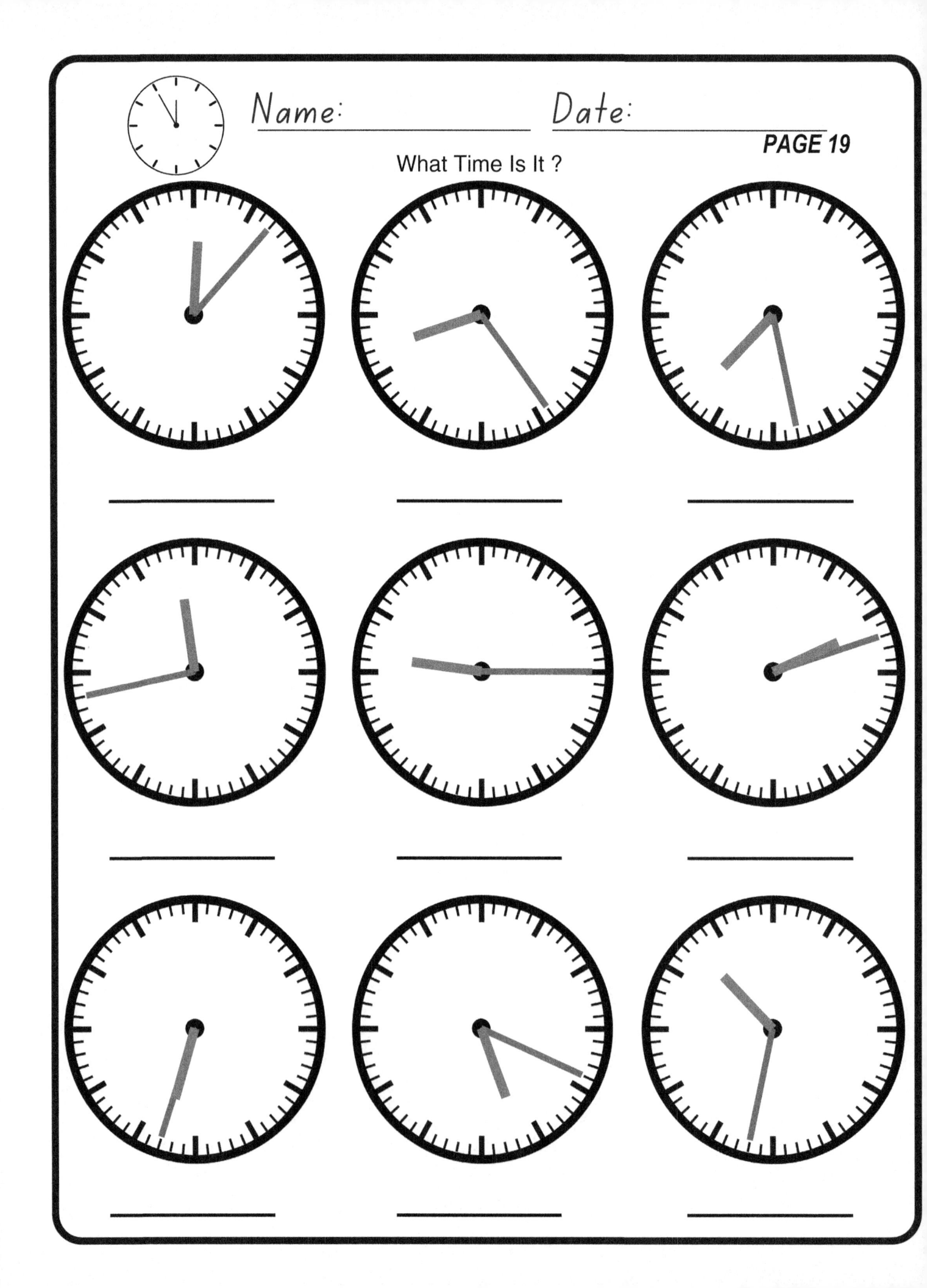

Name: _____ Date: _____

PAGE 19

What Time Is It ?

Name: _____ **Date:** _____

PAGE 20

Draw the Hands on the Clock Face

12:54	2:14	9:49
1:42	8:38	4:32
10:32	7:29	5:12

Name: _____ Date: _____

PAGE 21

What Time Is It ?

Name: _____ Date: _____

PAGE 22

Draw the Hands on the Clock Face

9:53	2:24	1:11

8:42	5:50	10:47

11:58	6:38	7:59

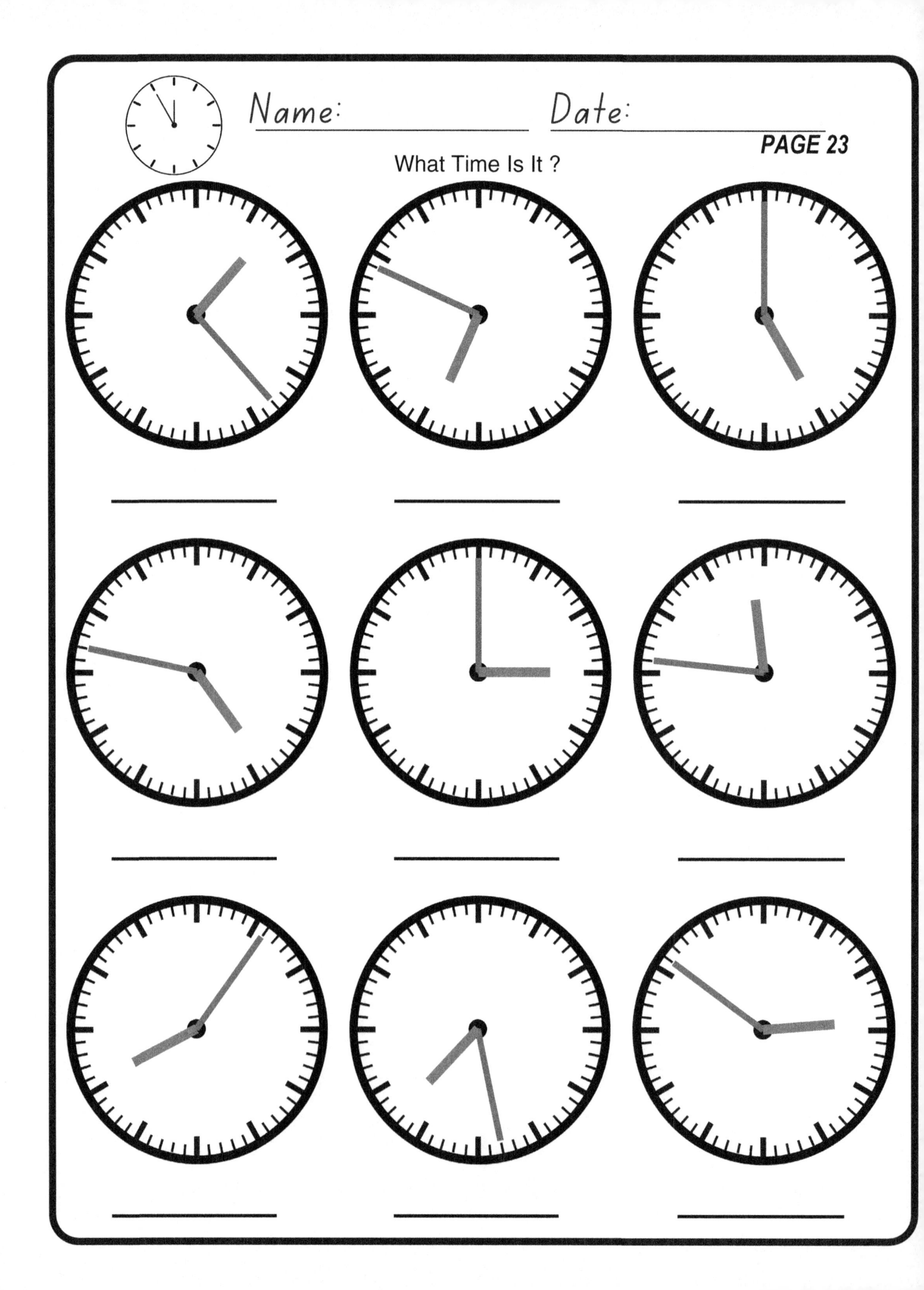

Name: Date:

PAGE 23

What Time Is It ?

Name: _____ Date: _____

PAGE 24

Draw the Hands on the Clock Face

6:28 4:06 3:37

1:42 5:09 2:43

9:42 11:25 8:47

PAGE 25

Matching Digital and Analog Clocks

Match the letter of each analog clock to a digital clock based on the time shown.

A.  PM — 3:30 PM

B.  PM — 8:30 PM

C.  PM — 5:15 AM

D.  PM — 10:45 PM

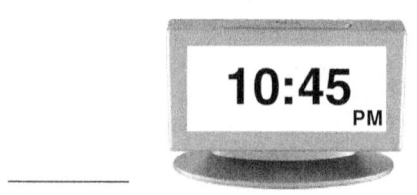

E.  AM — 2:15 PM

PAGE 26

Filling In Time On Clocks

Fill out each missing clock based off the time of its pair.

1) [clock showing ~9:15 PM] [blank digital clock]

2)  [blank analog clock] 1:00 AM

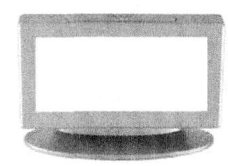

3) [clock showing ~8:15 PM] [blank digital clock]

4)  [clock showing ~12:20 AM] [blank digital clock]

5)  [blank analog clock] 8:30 PM

6)  [blank analog clock] 7:45 AM

7)  [blank analog clock] 10:15 AM

8)  [clock showing ~6:00 AM] [blank digital clock]

9) [clock showing ~9:10 PM] [blank digital clock]

10) [blank analog clock] 3:15 PM

PAGE 27

Matching Digital and Analog Clocks

Match the letter of each analog clock to a digital clock based on the time shown.

A.    AM   _____   9:30 AM

B.    AM   _____   8:00 AM

C.    PM   _____   11:20 PM

D.    PM   _____   7:40 PM

E.    PM   _____   2:50 PM

PAGE 28

Filling In Time On Clocks

Fill out each missing clock based off the time of its pair.

1)  5:10 PM

2)  PM

3) 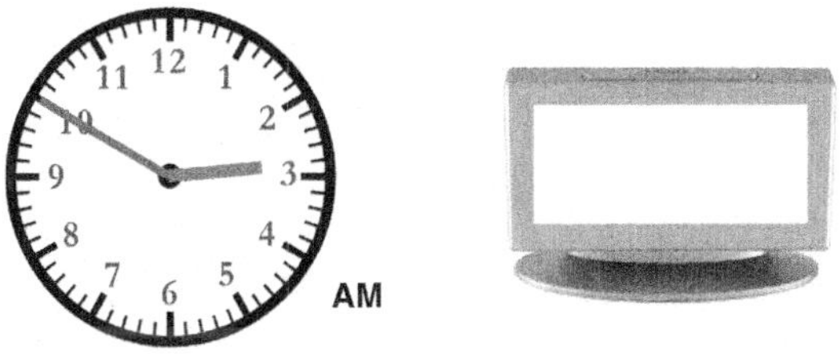 AM

4)  4:50 AM

5)  12:40 PM

6)  AM

7)  7:30 AM

8)  PM

9) 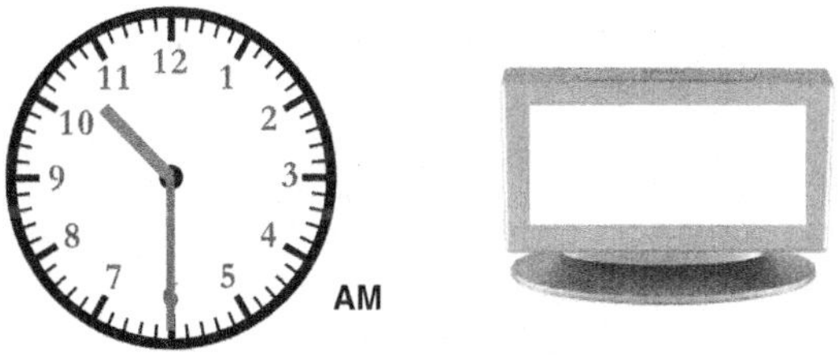 AM

10) 8:10 AM

PAGE 29

Matching Digital and Analog Clocks

Match the letter of each analog clock to a digital clock based on the time shown.

A.  AM — 9:30 AM

B.  AM — 8:00 AM

C.  PM — 11:20 PM

D.  PM — 7:40 PM

E.  PM — 2:50 PM

PAGE 30

Filling In Time On Clocks

Fill out each missing clock based off the time of its pair.

1)  5:10 PM

2)  PM

3) AM

4)  4:50 AM

5)  12:40 PM

6)  AM

7)  7:30 AM

8)  PM

9) 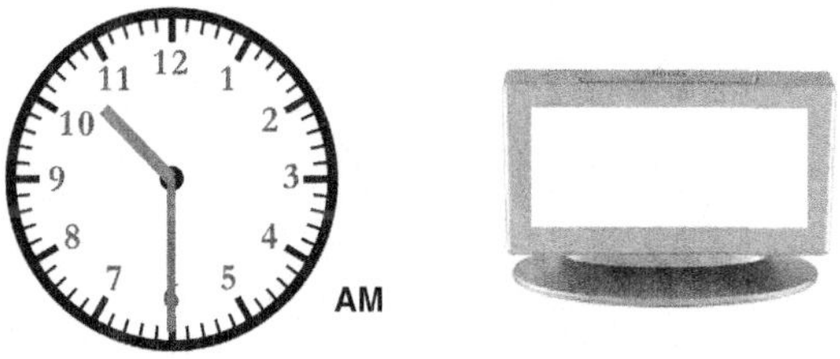 AM

10) 8:10 AM

PAGE 31

Matching Digital and Analog Clocks

Match the letter of each analog clock to a digital clock based on the time shown.

A.  AM — 1:15 AM

B.  AM — 10:10 PM

C.  PM — 11:45 PM

D.  AM — 6:20 AM

E.  PM — 5:35 AM

PAGE 32

Filling In Time On Clocks

Fill out each missing clock based off the time of its pair.

1)  [clock] 12:15 PM

2)  [clock] 8:10 PM

3)  [clock showing ~7:35] PM

4)  [clock showing ~10:22] PM

5)  [clock] 11:30 AM

6)  [clock] 5:50 PM

7)  [clock] 9:05 PM

8)  [clock showing ~9:10] AM

9) [clock showing ~6:55] PM

10) [clock showing ~8:14] AM

PAGE 33

Matching Digital and Analog Clocks

Match the letter of each analog clock to a digital clock based on the time shown.

A.  PM — 10:00 PM

B.  PM — 1:20 AM

C.  AM — 3:55 PM

D.  PM — 8:25 PM

E.  AM — 4:50 AM

Filling In Time On Clocks

Fill out each missing clock based off the time of its pair.

1)  11:50 PM

2)  AM

3)  PM

4)  3:15 AM

5)  4:30 AM

6) AM

7) 5:00 AM

8) PM

9) 9:40 AM

10)  AM

PAGE 34

Name: _____ Date: _____

PAGE 35

Matching Digital and Analog Clocks

Match the letter of each analog clock to a digital clock based on the time shown.

A. PM

B. AM

C. AM

D. PM

E. AM

6:19 PM ____

8:04 AM ____

9:47 AM ____

10:03 AM ____

11:18 PM ____

Name: ____________________ Date: ____________________

Filling In Time On Clocks

Fill out each missing clock based off the time of its pair.

1)

3:19
AM

2)

AM

3)

2:35
PM

4)

1:39
PM

5)

11:50
AM

6)

6:41
PM

7)

AM

8)

PM

9)

PM

10)

AM

Matching Digital and Analog Clocks

Match the letter of each analog clock to a digital clock based on the time shown.

A.  AM

B.  AM

C.  PM

D.  PM

E.  AM

8:02 AM ____

5:32 AM ____

6:37 PM ____

2:38 AM ____

12:33 PM ____

PAGE 37

Name: ____________________ Date: ____________________

Filling In Time On Clocks

Fill out each missing clock based off the time of its pair.

1) 
PM

6) 
10:09
AM

2) 
3:56
AM

7) 
AM

3) 
PM

8) 
PM

4) 
7:36
PM

9) 
11:40
AM

5) 
AM

10) 
1:24
AM

PAGE 39

Matching Digital and Analog Clocks

Match the letter of each analog clock to a digital clock based on the time shown.

A.  [analog clock] AM — [digital] 12:54 PM

B. [analog clock] PM — [digital] 6:48 AM

C.  [analog clock] PM — [digital] 10:35 PM

D.  [analog clock] PM — [digital] 4:45 AM

E. [analog clock] AM — [digital] 5:20 PM

PAGE 40

Filling In Time On Clocks

Fill out each missing clock based off the time of its pair.

1)   10:18 PM

2)   4:35 PM

3)  PM

4)  PM

5)  AM

6)  AM

7)   9:58 AM

8)   2:29 AM

9)  PM

10)   6:27 AM

Name: _____ Date: _____

PAGE 41

What time is on the clock? _____

What time will it be in 4 hours? _____

What time was it 1 hour ago? _____

What time will it be in 2 hours? _____

What time is on the clock? _____

What time was it 3 hours ago? _____

What time was it 4 hours ago? _____

What time will it be in 2 hours? _____

What time is on the clock? _____

What time was it 4 hours ago? _____

What time will it be in 1 hour? _____

What time was it 2 hours ago? _____

What time is on the clock? _____

What time will it be in 2 hours? _____

What time was it 1 hour ago? _____

What time was it 4 hours ago? _____

Name: _____ Date: _____

PAGE 42

What time is on the clock? _____

What time will it be in 2 hours? _____

What time was it 3 hours ago? _____

What time will it be in 4 hours? _____

What time is on the clock? _____

What time will it be in 3 hours? _____

What time was it 1 hour ago? _____

What time was it 5 hours ago? _____

What time is on the clock? _____

What time will it be in 3 hours? _____

What time was it 1 hour ago? _____

What time will it be in 2 hours? _____

What time is on the clock? _____

What time was it 4 hours ago? _____

What time will it be in 5 hours? _____

What time will it be in 3 hours? _____

Name: _____ Date: _____

PAGE 43

What time is on the clock? _____

What time was it 120 minutes ago? _____

What time will it be in 90 minutes? _____

What time was it 30 minutes ago? _____

What time is on the clock? _____

What time was it 90 minutes ago? _____

What time will it be in 30 minutes? _____

What time will it be in 120 minutes? _____

What time is on the clock? _____

What time will it be in 60 minutes? _____

What time was it 120 minutes ago? _____

What time will it be in 30 minutes? _____

What time is on the clock? _____

What time will it be in 90 minutes? _____

What time will it be in 120 minutes? _____

What time was it 30 minutes ago? _____

Name: _____ Date: _____

PAGE 44

What time is on the clock? _____

What time was it 40 minutes ago? _____

What time will it be in 80 minutes? _____

What time will it be in 20 minutes? _____

What time is on the clock? _____

What time was it 100 minutes ago? _____

What time will it be in 20 minutes? _____

What time was it 60 minutes ago? _____

What time is on the clock? _____

What time will it be in 80 minutes? _____

What time will it be in 100 minutes? _____

What time was it 40 minutes ago? _____

What time is on the clock? _____

What time was it 40 minutes ago? _____

What time was it 80 minutes ago? _____

What time will it be in 60 minutes? _____

Name: _____ Date: _____

PAGE 45

What time is on the clock? _____

What time was it 15 minutes ago? _____

What time will it be in 30 minutes? _____

What time will it be in 90 minutes? _____

What time is on the clock? _____

What time was it 90 minutes ago? _____

What time was it 30 minutes ago? _____

What time will it be in 75 minutes? _____

What time is on the clock? _____

What time will it be in 45 minutes? _____

What time was it 30 minutes ago? _____

What time was it 75 minutes ago? _____

What time is on the clock? _____

What time will it be in 30 minutes? _____

What time was it 90 minutes ago? _____

What time was it 60 minutes ago? _____

Name: _____ Date: _____

PAGE 46

What time is on the clock? _____

What time will it be in 70 minutes? _____

What time was it 60 minutes ago? _____

What time was it 30 minutes ago? _____

What time is on the clock? _____

What time was it 80 minutes ago? _____

What time will it be in 50 minutes? _____

What time will it be in 40 minutes? _____

What time is on the clock? _____

What time was it 60 minutes ago? _____

What time will it be in 20 minutes? _____

What time was it 70 minutes ago? _____

What time is on the clock? _____

What time will it be in 80 minutes? _____

What time was it 50 minutes ago? _____

What time will it be in 30 minutes? _____

Name: _____ Date: _____

PAGE 47

What time is on the clock? _____

What time was it 50 minutes ago? _____

What time will it be in 45 minutes? _____

What time was it 35 minutes ago? _____

What time is on the clock? _____

What time will it be in 60 minutes? _____

What time will it be in 45 minutes? _____

What time was it 35 minutes ago? _____

What time is on the clock? _____

What time was it 50 minutes ago? _____

What time was it 30 minutes ago? _____

What time will it be in 40 minutes? _____

What time is on the clock? _____

What time will it be in 40 minutes? _____

What time will it be in 30 minutes? _____

What time was it 55 minutes ago? _____

Name: _____ Date: _____

PAGE 48

What time is on the clock? _____

What time will it be in 11 minutes? _____

What time was it 35 minutes ago? _____

What time was it 23 minutes ago? _____

What time is on the clock? _____

What time will it be in 54 minutes? _____

What time was it 36 minutes ago? _____

What time was it 58 minutes ago? _____

What time is on the clock? _____

What time was it 47 minutes ago? _____

What time was it 26 minutes ago? _____

What time will it be in 15 minutes? _____

What time is on the clock? _____

What time will it be in 19 minutes? _____

What time was it 11 minutes ago? _____

What time will it be in 61 minutes? _____

Name: _____ Date: _____

PAGE 49

What time is on the clock? _____

What time was it 3 hours and 30 minutes ago? _____

What time was it 1 hour and 30 minutes ago? _____

What time will it be in 4 hours? _____

What time is on the clock? _____

What time was it 2 hours ago? _____

What time will it be in 1 hour and 30 minutes? _____

What time will it be in 3 hours and 30 minutes? _____

What time is on the clock? _____

What time will it be in 3 hours and 30 minutes? _____

What time was it 2 hours and 30 minutes ago? _____

What time was it 1 hour ago? _____

What time is on the clock? _____

What time will it be in 4 hours? _____

What time will it be in 2 hours and 30 minutes? _____

What time was it 3 hours ago? _____

Name: _____ Date: _____

PAGE 50

What time is on the clock? _____

What time will it be in 4 hours and 30 minutes? _____

What time will it be in 2 hours ? _____

What time was it 1 hour and 45 minutes ago? _____

What time is on the clock? _____

What time will it be in 2 hours and 15 minutes? _____

What time was it 3 hours ago? _____

What time was it 4 hours and 30 minutes ago? _____

What time is on the clock? _____

What time will it be in 2 hours and 15 minutes? _____

What time was it 4 hours and 30 minutes ago? _____

What time was it 3 hours and 45 minutes ago? _____

What time is on the clock? _____

What time will it be in 3 hours ? _____

What time was it 4 hours and 15 minutes ago? _____

What time will it be in 1 hour and 30 minutes? _____

Name: _____ Date: _____

PAGE 51

What time is on the clock? _____

What time will it be in 2 hours and 59 minutes? _____

What time will it be in 5 hours and 39 minutes? _____

What time was it 8 hours and 30 minutes ago? _____

What time is on the clock? _____

What time will it be in 6 hours and 29 minutes? _____

What time was it 3 hours and 42 minutes ago? _____

What time was it 4 hours and 55 minutes ago? _____

What time is on the clock? _____

What time was it 7 hours and 33 minutes ago? _____

What time will it be in 1 hour and 45 minutes? _____

What time will it be in 6 hours and 13 minutes? _____

What time is on the clock? _____

What time will it be in 9 hours and 44 minutes? _____

What time was it 2 hours and 33 minutes ago? _____

What time will it be in 3 hours and 39 minutes? _____

Name: _____ Date: _____

PAGE 52

What time is on the clock? _____

What time was it 8 hours and 25 minutes ago? _____

What time will it be in 7 hours and 21 minutes? _____

What time will it be in 4 hours and 23 minutes? _____

What time is on the clock? _____

What time was it 8 hours and 45 minutes ago? _____

What time was it 7 hours and 30 minutes ago? _____

What time will it be in 5 hours and 46 minutes? _____

What time is on the clock? _____

What time will it be in 8 hours and 56 minutes? _____

What time was it 4 hours and 52 minutes ago? _____

What time was it 9 hours and 16 minutes ago? _____

What time is on the clock? _____

What time will it be in 9 hours and 46 minutes? _____

What time will it be in 5 hours ? _____

What time was it 4 hours and 31 minutes ago? _____

Name: _____ Date: _____

PAGE 53

What time is on Clock A ? _____

What time is on Clock B ? _____

How much time has elapsed between Clock A and B ? _____

Clock A   Clock B

What time is on Clock A ? _____

What time is on Clock B ? _____

How much time has elapsed between Clock A and B ? _____

Clock A   Clock B

What time is on Clock A ? _____

What time is on Clock B ? _____

How much time has elapsed between Clock A and B ? _____

Clock A   Clock B

What time is on Clock A ? _____

What time is on Clock B ? _____

How much time has elapsed between Clock A and B ? _____

Clock A   Clock B

Name: _____ **Date:** _____

PAGE 54

How Much Time Has Elapsed ?

1) 10:30 P.M. to 1:30 A.M. _____

2) 10:30 A.M. to 3:30 P.M. _____

3) 4:30 A.M. to 9:30 A.M. _____

4) 1:00 A.M. to 5:00 A.M. _____

5) 1:00 A.M. to 4:00 A.M. _____

6) 10:30 A.M. to 1:30 P.M. _____

7) 9:00 P.M. to 10:00 P.M. _____

8) 1:00 P.M. to 3:00 P.M. _____

9) 2:00 A.M. to 7:00 A.M. _____

10) 11:30 P.M. to 4:30 A.M. _____

11) 6:00 P.M. to 10:00 P.M. _____

12) 11:30 P.M. to 1:30 A.M. _____

13) 9:30 A.M. to 12:30 P.M. _____

14) 3:00 A.M. to 5:00 A.M. _____

15) 6:00 P.M. to 11:00 P.M. _____

Name: _____ **Date:** _____

PAGE 55

Clock A Clock B
What time is on Clock A ? _____
What time is on Clock B ? _____
How much time has elapsed between Clock A and B ? _____

Clock A Clock B
What time is on Clock A ? _____
What time is on Clock B ? _____
How much time has elapsed between Clock A and B ? _____

Clock A Clock B
What time is on Clock A ? _____
What time is on Clock B ? _____
How much time has elapsed between Clock A and B ? _____

Clock A Clock B
What time is on Clock A ? _____
What time is on Clock B ? _____
How much time has elapsed between Clock A and B ? _____

Name: _____ Date: _____

PAGE 56

How Much Time Has Elapsed ?

1)   5:30 A.M.   to   10:30 A.M.   _____

2)   10:00 A.M. to   11:00 A.M.   _____

3)   8:30 P.M.   to   11:30 P.M.   _____

4)   11:00 A.M. to   2:00 P.M.   _____

5)   5:00 P.M.   to   9:00 P.M.   _____

6)   2:00 A.M.   to   4:00 A.M.   _____

7)   2:00 P.M.   to   7:00 P.M.   _____

8)   12:30 P.M. to   2:30 P.M.   _____

9)   8:00 P.M.   to   12:00 A.M.   _____

10) 8:00 P.M.   to   10:00 P.M.   _____

11) 5:30 A.M.   to   7:30 A.M.   _____

12) 5:30 P.M.   to   10:30 P.M.   _____

13) 12:00 P.M. to   5:00 P.M.   _____

14) 3:00 P.M.   to   7:00 P.M.   _____

15) 4:00 A.M.   to   6:00 A.M.   _____

Name: _____ Date: _____

PAGE 57

Clock A / **Clock B**

What time is on Clock A ? _____

What time is on Clock B ? _____

How much time has elapsed between Clock A and B ? _____

Clock A / **Clock B**

What time is on Clock A ? _____

What time is on Clock B ? _____

How much time has elapsed between Clock A and B ? _____

Clock A / **Clock B**

What time is on Clock A ? _____

What time is on Clock B ? _____

How much time has elapsed between Clock A and B ? _____

Clock A / **Clock B**

What time is on Clock A ? _____

What time is on Clock B ? _____

How much time has elapsed between Clock A and B ? _____

Name: _____ Date: _____

PAGE 58

How Much Time Has Elapsed ?

1) 2:00 P.M. to 6:00 P.M. _____

2) 2:30 A.M. to 4:30 A.M. _____

3) 6:00 A.M. to 10:00 A.M. _____

4) 2:30 P.M. to 4:30 P.M. _____

5) 10:30 P.M. to 1:30 A.M. _____

6) 8:00 A.M. to 12:00 P.M. _____

7) 3:30 A.M. to 5:30 A.M. _____

8) 4:00 A.M. to 8:00 A.M. _____

9) 11:00 A.M. to 1:00 P.M. _____

10) 11:30 P.M. to 2:30 A.M. _____

11) 9:30 A.M. to 11:30 A.M. _____

12) 9:00 P.M. to 12:00 A.M. _____

13) 5:30 A.M. to 6:30 A.M. _____

14) 2:00 P.M. to 3:00 P.M. _____

15) 7:00 P.M. to 11:00 P.M. _____

Name: _____ Date: _____

PAGE 59

Clock A Clock B

What time is on Clock A ? _____

What time is on Clock B ? _____

How much time has elapsed between Clock A and B ? _____

Clock A Clock B

What time is on Clock A ? _____

What time is on Clock B ? _____

How much time has elapsed between Clock A and B ? _____

Clock A Clock B

What time is on Clock A ? _____

What time is on Clock B ? _____

How much time has elapsed between Clock A and B ? _____

Clock A Clock B

What time is on Clock A ? _____

What time is on Clock B ? _____

How much time has elapsed between Clock A and B ? _____

Name: _____ Date: _____

PAGE 60

How Much Time Has Elapsed ?

1)   2:15 A.M.   to   2:36 A.M.   _____

2)   4:15 A.M.   to   5:14 A.M.   _____

3)   12:15 P.M. to   1:05 P.M.   _____

4)   11:00 A.M. to   11:41 A.M. _____

5)   9:30 A.M.   to   9:46 A.M.   _____

6)   6:15 P.M.   to   7:04 P.M.   _____

7)   6:45 P.M.   to   7:39 P.M.   _____

8)   7:00 P.M.   to   7:36 P.M.   _____

9)   5:15 A.M.   to   5:47 A.M.   _____

10) 12:15 A.M. to   12:59 A.M. _____

11) 5:00 P.M.   to   5:35 P.M.   _____

12) 3:15 P.M.   to   3:30 P.M.   _____

13) 9:45 A.M.   to   10:13 A.M. _____

14) 8:45 P.M.   to   9:06 P.M.   _____

15) 6:00 A.M.   to   6:53 A.M.   _____

Name: _____ Date: _____

PAGE 61

Clock A | Clock B | What time is on Clock A? _____
 | | What time is on Clock B? _____
 | | How much time has elapsed between Clock A and B? _____

Clock A | Clock B | What time is on Clock A? _____
 | | What time is on Clock B? _____
 | | How much time has elapsed between Clock A and B? _____

Clock A | Clock B | What time is on Clock A? _____
 | | What time is on Clock B? _____
 | | How much time has elapsed between Clock A and B? _____

Clock A | Clock B | What time is on Clock A? _____
 | | What time is on Clock B? _____
 | | How much time has elapsed between Clock A and B? _____

Name: _____ Date: _____

PAGE 62

How Much Time Has Elapsed?

1) 3:25 P.M. to 4:00 P.M. _____

2) 7:00 A.M. to 7:13 A.M. _____

3) 12:10 A.M. to 12:26 A.M. _____

4) 3:30 P.M. to 4:07 P.M. _____

5) 12:10 P.M. to 12:21 P.M. _____

6) 8:25 A.M. to 8:58 A.M. _____

7) 6:30 P.M. to 6:55 P.M. _____

8) 9:30 A.M. to 10:07 A.M. _____

9) 11:55 P.M. to 12:52 A.M. _____

10) 7:35 P.M. to 8:09 P.M. _____

11) 2:35 A.M. to 3:17 A.M. _____

12) 1:25 A.M. to 2:03 A.M. _____

13) 7:20 A.M. to 8:05 A.M. _____

14) 1:50 P.M. to 2:29 P.M. _____

15) 12:50 P.M. to 1:29 P.M. _____

Name: _____ Date: _____

PAGE 63

Clock A   Clock B

What time is on Clock A ? _____

What time is on Clock B ? _____

How much time has elapsed between Clock A and B ? _____

Clock A   Clock B

What time is on Clock A ? _____

What time is on Clock B ? _____

How much time has elapsed between Clock A and B ? _____

Clock A   Clock B

What time is on Clock A ? _____

What time is on Clock B ? _____

How much time has elapsed between Clock A and B ? _____

Clock A   Clock B

What time is on Clock A ? _____

What time is on Clock B ? _____

How much time has elapsed between Clock A and B ? _____

Name: _____ Date: _____

PAGE 64

How Much Time Has Elapsed ?

1)   8:05 P.M.   to   8:32 P.M.   _____

2)   7:00 A.M.   to   7:55 A.M.   _____

3)   3:05 A.M.   to   4:03 A.M.   _____

4)   1:20 P.M.   to   1:54 P.M.   _____

5)   11:00 A.M.   to   11:19 A.M.   _____

6)   5:50 P.M.   to   6:12 P.M.   _____

7)   8:30 A.M.   to   9:23 A.M.   _____

8)   2:30 A.M.   to   3:02 A.M.   _____

9)   6:15 P.M.   to   6:58 P.M.   _____

10)   5:35 P.M.   to   6:21 P.M.   _____

11)   11:05 A.M.   to   11:44 A.M.   _____

12)   2:00 P.M.   to   2:18 P.M.   _____

13)   7:50 A.M.   to   8:35 A.M.   _____

14)   11:10 A.M.   to   11:26 A.M.   _____

15)   6:40 P.M.   to   7:35 P.M.   _____

Name: _____ Date: _____

PAGE 65

Clock A   Clock B

What time is on Clock A? _____
What time is on Clock B? _____
How much time has elapsed between Clock A and B? _____

Clock A   Clock B

What time is on Clock A? _____
What time is on Clock B? _____
How much time has elapsed between Clock A and B? _____

Clock A   Clock B

What time is on Clock A? _____
What time is on Clock B? _____
How much time has elapsed between Clock A and B? _____

Clock A   Clock B

What time is on Clock A? _____
What time is on Clock B? _____
How much time has elapsed between Clock A and B? _____

Name: _____ Date: _____

PAGE 66

How Much Time Has Elapsed ?

1) 4:00 P.M. to 5:55 P.M. _____

2) 6:20 A.M. to 10:13 A.M. _____

3) 3:40 P.M. to 4:51 P.M. _____

4) 3:00 P.M. to 5:54 P.M. _____

5) 5:00 P.M. to 6:29 P.M. _____

6) 2:40 A.M. to 4:37 A.M. _____

7) 10:40 A.M. to 3:25 P.M. _____

8) 9:40 A.M. to 11:31 A.M. _____

9) 5:00 A.M. to 8:56 A.M. _____

10) 4:20 P.M. to 8:08 P.M. _____

11) 3:20 P.M. to 4:31 P.M. _____

12) 10:00 A.M. to 1:18 P.M. _____

13) 10:40 P.M. to 1:10 A.M. _____

14) 12:00 A.M. to 2:51 A.M. _____

15) 5:00 A.M. to 6:31 A.M. _____

Name: _____ Date: _____

PAGE 67

Clock A Clock B

What time is on Clock A? _____

What time is on Clock B? _____

How much time has elapsed between Clock A and B? _____

Clock A Clock B

What time is on Clock A? _____

What time is on Clock B? _____

How much time has elapsed between Clock A and B? _____

Clock A Clock B

What time is on Clock A? _____

What time is on Clock B? _____

How much time has elapsed between Clock A and B? _____

Clock A Clock B

What time is on Clock A? _____

What time is on Clock B? _____

How much time has elapsed between Clock A and B? _____

Name: _____ Date: _____

PAGE 68

How Much Time Has Elapsed ?

1) 3:35 A.M. to 8:14 A.M. _____

2) 6:10 P.M. to 8:33 P.M. _____

3) 12:20 A.M. to 1:49 A.M. _____

4) 8:25 P.M. to 11:08 P.M. _____

5) 7:20 A.M. to 12:08 P.M. _____

6) 9:55 A.M. to 2:53 P.M. _____

7) 4:35 A.M. to 9:12 A.M. _____

8) 5:10 A.M. to 7:43 A.M. _____

9) 7:30 A.M. to 11:42 A.M. _____

10) 3:55 P.M. to 8:49 P.M. _____

11) 2:30 A.M. to 3:42 A.M. _____

12) 10:30 P.M. to 3:20 A.M. _____

13) 7:30 P.M. to 9:00 P.M. _____

14) 3:10 A.M. to 6:49 A.M. _____

15) 7:45 P.M. to 12:34 A.M. _____

Name: _____ **Date:** _____

PAGE 69

Clock A | Clock B

What time is on Clock A ? _____

What time is on Clock B ? _____

How much time has elapsed between Clock A and B ? _____

Clock A | Clock B

What time is on Clock A ? _____

What time is on Clock B ? _____

How much time has elapsed between Clock A and B ? _____

Clock A | Clock B

What time is on Clock A ? _____

What time is on Clock B ? _____

How much time has elapsed between Clock A and B ? _____

Clock A | Clock B

What time is on Clock A ? _____

What time is on Clock B ? _____

How much time has elapsed between Clock A and B ? _____

Name: _____ Date: _____

PAGE 70

How Much Time Has Elapsed ?

1) 3:40 P.M. to 6:51 P.M. _____

2) 4:50 A.M. to 6:00 A.M. _____

3) 3:05 P.M. to 8:04 P.M. _____

4) 3:00 A.M. to 4:46 A.M. _____

5) 4:10 A.M. to 6:55 A.M. _____

6) 7:30 P.M. to 11:05 P.M. _____

7) 6:00 A.M. to 9:11 A.M. _____

8) 2:10 A.M. to 6:39 A.M. _____

9) 5:00 P.M. to 9:50 P.M. _____

10) 9:15 A.M. to 11:41 A.M. _____

11) 11:50 P.M. to 1:11 A.M. _____

12) 1:45 P.M. to 6:18 P.M. _____

13) 2:15 P.M. to 3:52 P.M. _____

14) 7:45 P.M. to 9:24 P.M. _____

15) 5:35 P.M. to 8:26 P.M. _____

Name: _____ Date: _____

PAGE 71

Clock A   Clock B   What time is on Clock A ? _____

                              What time is on Clock B ? _____

                              How much time has elapsed
                              between Clock A and B ? _____

Clock A   Clock B   What time is on Clock A ? _____

                              What time is on Clock B ? _____

                              How much time has elapsed
                              between Clock A and B ? _____

Clock A   Clock B   What time is on Clock A ? _____

                              What time is on Clock B ? _____

                              How much time has elapsed
                              between Clock A and B ? _____

Clock A   Clock B   What time is on Clock A ? _____

                              What time is on Clock B ? _____

                              How much time has elapsed
                              between Clock A and B ? _____

Name: _____ Date: _____

PAGE 72

How Much Time Has Elapsed ?

1)   7:35 P.M.   to   8:54 P.M.   _____

2)   4:30 A.M.   to   7:57 A.M.   _____

3)   8:05 A.M.   to   11:23 A.M.   _____

4)   2:10 P.M.   to   5:02 P.M.   _____

5)   4:45 A.M.   to   8:56 A.M.   _____

6)   1:00 P.M.   to   2:18 P.M.   _____

7)   4:40 P.M.   to   8:15 P.M.   _____

8)   11:25 P.M.   to   2:40 A.M.   _____

9)   9:10 P.M.   to   10:40 P.M.   _____

10)   5:10 A.M.   to   9:37 A.M.   _____

11)   6:10 A.M.   to   8:21 A.M.   _____

12)   12:10 P.M.   to   3:06 P.M.   _____

13)   1:20 A.M.   to   5:04 A.M.   _____

14)   4:00 P.M.   to   6:45 P.M.   _____

15)   1:40 A.M.   to   5:08 A.M.   _____

Name: _____ Date: _____

PAGE 73

Clock A Clock B

What time is on Clock A? _____

What time is on Clock B? _____

How much time has elapsed between Clock A and B? _____

Clock A Clock B

What time is on Clock A? _____

What time is on Clock B? _____

How much time has elapsed between Clock A and B? _____

Clock A Clock B

What time is on Clock A? _____

What time is on Clock B? _____

How much time has elapsed between Clock A and B? _____

Clock A Clock B

What time is on Clock A? _____

What time is on Clock B? _____

How much time has elapsed between Clock A and B? _____

Name: _____ Date: _____

PAGE 74

How Much Time Has Elapsed ?

1)   6:25 A.M.   to   9:10 A.M.   _____

2)   7:01 A.M.   to   12:50 P.M.   _____

3)   1:13 P.M.   to   2:42 P.M.   _____

4)   8:13 A.M.   to   4:59 P.M.   _____

5)   2:01 P.M.   to   10:18 P.M.   _____

6)   5:43 A.M.   to   11:38 A.M.   _____

7)   5:09 A.M.   to   1:45 P.M.   _____

8)   11:59 P.M.   to   9:51 A.M.   _____

9)   9:00 A.M.   to   10:41 A.M.   _____

10)   9:54 P.M.   to   6:40 A.M.   _____

11)   8:19 P.M.   to   12:02 A.M.   _____

12)   10:34 P.M.   to   2:17 A.M.   _____

13)   1:41 A.M.   to   11:28 A.M.   _____

14)   11:32 P.M.   to   12:57 A.M.   _____

15)   2:41 P.M.   to   9:19 P.M.   _____

Name: _____ Date: _____

PAGE 75

What time is on Clock A ? _____

What time is on Clock B ? _____

How much time has elapsed between Clock A and B ? _____

Clock A   Clock B

What time is on Clock A ? _____

What time is on Clock B ? _____

How much time has elapsed between Clock A and B ? _____

Clock A   Clock B

What time is on Clock A ? _____

What time is on Clock B ? _____

How much time has elapsed between Clock A and B ? _____

Clock A   Clock B

What time is on Clock A ? _____

What time is on Clock B ? _____

How much time has elapsed between Clock A and B ? _____

Clock A   Clock B

Name: _____ Date: _____

PAGE 76

How Much Time Has Elapsed ?

1)   4:50 P.M.   to   2:03 A.M.   _____

2)   1:18 A.M.   to   5:49 A.M.   _____

3)   6:03 A.M.   to   8:22 A.M.   _____

4) 11:26 P.M.   to   1:22 A.M.   _____

5) 11:00 A.M.   to   4:52 P.M.   _____

6)   9:21 A.M.   to   4:13 P.M.   _____

7)   2:07 A.M.   to   3:58 A.M.   _____

8) 10:35 A.M.   to   5:16 P.M.   _____

9)   5:52 P.M.   to 12:08 A.M.   _____

10) 11:50 A.M.   to   4:35 P.M.   _____

11)   6:16 A.M.   to   3:26 P.M.   _____

12) 12:16 P.M.   to   6:08 P.M.   _____

13)   9:16 P.M.   to   3:35 A.M.   _____

14)   1:05 P.M.   to   5:25 P.M.   _____

15)   3:30 P.M.   to 12:10 A.M.   _____

Name: _____ Date: _____

PAGE 77

Complete the Table Below.

Start Time	End Time	Elapsed Time
1:00 P.M.	4:00 P.M.	
	12:20 P.M.	1 Hours & 0 Minutes
	5:00 A.M.	5 Hours & 0 Minutes
	3:40 A.M.	1 Hours & 0 Minutes
	11:40 P.M.	2 Hours & 0 Minutes
	9:00 A.M.	1 Hours & 0 Minutes
	6:00 P.M.	5 Hours & 0 Minutes
2:40 P.M.		4 Hours & 0 Minutes
	4:00 P.M.	5 Hours & 0 Minutes
3:40 P.M.		4 Hours & 0 Minutes

Name: _____ Date: _____

PAGE 78

Complete the Table Below.

Start Time	End Time	Elapsed Time
3:35 A.M.		1 Hours & 0 Minutes
3:15 A.M.		4 Hours & 0 Minutes
2:10 A.M.		2 Hours & 0 Minutes
	5:40 P.M.	4 Hours & 0 Minutes
3:20 P.M.		2 Hours & 0 Minutes
10:10 A.M.		1 Hours & 0 Minutes
	12:55 P.M.	5 Hours & 0 Minutes
6:50 P.M.	9:50 P.M.	
10:40 A.M.	11:40 A.M.	
	3:10 P.M.	5 Hours & 0 Minutes

Name: _____ Date: _____

PAGE 79

Complete the Table Below.

Start Time	End Time	Elapsed Time
5:05 A.M.		0 Hours & 21 Minutes
5:25 A.M.		0 Hours & 41 Minutes
	8:17 A.M.	0 Hours & 12 Minutes
	4:26 P.M.	0 Hours & 46 Minutes
	3:41 P.M.	0 Hours & 26 Minutes
	5:21 P.M.	0 Hours & 16 Minutes
	3:37 P.M.	0 Hours & 22 Minutes
8:45 P.M.	9:21 P.M.	
12:35 A.M.	12:51 A.M.	
3:05 A.M.		0 Hours & 32 Minutes

Name: _____ Date: _____

PAGE 80

Complete the Table Below.

Start Time	End Time	Elapsed Time
7:25 P.M.		0 Hours & 36 Minutes
	8:34 P.M.	0 Hours & 29 Minutes
1:50 P.M.		0 Hours & 52 Minutes
3:45 P.M.		0 Hours & 15 Minutes
	1:18 A.M.	0 Hours & 28 Minutes
	5:19 A.M.	0 Hours & 29 Minutes
7:00 A.M.		0 Hours & 39 Minutes
4:20 P.M.		0 Hours & 17 Minutes
8:20 A.M.		0 Hours & 59 Minutes
6:15 P.M.	7:00 P.M.	

Name: _____ Date: _____

PAGE 81

Complete the Table Below.

Start Time	End Time	Elapsed Time
4:40 P.M.	7:26 P.M.	
3:10 P.M.		4 Hours & 53 Minutes
4:55 A.M.	7:36 A.M.	
10:55 A.M.	3:10 P.M.	
4:15 A.M.	9:06 A.M.	
	7:23 P.M.	4 Hours & 23 Minutes
	1:18 A.M.	2 Hours & 43 Minutes
7:10 P.M.		1 Hours & 53 Minutes
9:40 A.M.		3 Hours & 14 Minutes
2:35 P.M.		4 Hours & 28 Minutes

Name: _____ Date: _____

PAGE 82

Complete the Table Below.

Start Time	End Time	Elapsed Time
	12:01 A.M.	3 Hours & 46 Minutes
4:25 A.M.		2 Hours & 57 Minutes
	11:47 A.M.	3 Hours & 17 Minutes
	1:07 P.M.	4 Hours & 37 Minutes
3:55 P.M.		1 Hours & 37 Minutes
	12:10 A.M.	2 Hours & 30 Minutes
	12:54 P.M.	4 Hours & 59 Minutes
	7:28 A.M.	3 Hours & 18 Minutes
1:20 P.M.		2 Hours & 33 Minutes
7:40 P.M.		3 Hours & 24 Minutes

Name: _____ Date: _____

PAGE 83

Complete the Table Below.

Start Time	End Time	Elapsed Time
4:05 P.M.	8:02 P.M.	
	12:32 P.M.	4 Hours & 22 Minutes
11:05 P.M.	12:26 A.M.	
	11:59 A.M.	3 Hours & 34 Minutes
2:30 A.M.	5:40 A.M.	
	2:45 P.M.	2 Hours & 15 Minutes
3:15 A.M.		2 Hours & 17 Minutes
	5:07 A.M.	3 Hours & 37 Minutes
	6:48 A.M.	3 Hours & 28 Minutes
12:45 A.M.		1 Hours & 16 Minutes

Name: _____ **Date:** _____

PAGE 84

Complete the Table Below.

Start Time	End Time	Elapsed Time
1:45 A.M.	5:00 A.M.	
11:20 A.M.	3:04 P.M.	
7:55 P.M.		2 Hours & 58 Minutes
	4:21 A.M.	2 Hours & 31 Minutes
	5:55 A.M.	1 Hours & 20 Minutes
2:00 A.M.		2 Hours & 12 Minutes
9:50 A.M.		4 Hours & 49 Minutes
1:05 A.M.	3:00 A.M.	
11:00 P.M.	3:57 A.M.	
3:25 P.M.		1 Hours & 23 Minutes

Name: _____ Date: _____

PAGE 85

1) _____ Seconds = 1 Minute
2) 30 Minutes = _____ Hour
3) _____ Minutes = 1 Hour
4) 365 _____ = 1 Year
5) 365 Days = _____ Year
6) 15 _____ = 1/4 Hour
7) 60 Minutes = 1 _____
8) 12 Months = 1 _____
9) 7 Days = _____ Week
10) 365 Days = _____ Year
11) 1 _____ = 60 Seconds
12) 1 Minute = _____ Seconds
13) _____ Minutes = 1 Hour
14) 15 Minutes = 1 _____
15) 365 Days = _____ Year
16) 52 _____ = 1 Year
17) 24 Hours = 1 _____
18) 30 Minutes = 1/2 _____
19) 1 Minute = 60 _____
20) _____ Minute = 60 Seconds

1) 30 Minutes = 1/2 _____
2) 12 Months = 1 _____
3) 60 Seconds = _____ Minute
4) 52 Weeks = 1 _____
5) 60 Seconds = _____ Minute
6) 60 _____ = 1 Hour
7) _____ Minute = 60 Seconds
8) 60 _____ = 1 Hour
9) 7 Days = _____ Week
10) 7 Days = _____ Week
11) 52 Weeks = _____ Year
12) _____ Minutes = 1/4 Hour
13) 365 _____ = 1 Year
14) _____ Minutes = 1/4 Hour
15) 24 _____ = 1 Day
16) _____ Seconds = 1 Minute
17) 15 Minutes = 1 _____
18) 60 Minutes = 1 _____
19) 24 Hours = 1 _____
20) 60 Minutes = 1 _____

Name: _____ Date: _____

PAGE 86

1) 60 Minutes = 1 _____
2) 7 _____ = 1 Week
3) 7 Days = ____ Week
4) 12 Months = ____ Year
5) ____ Months = 1 Year
6) 12 Months = 1 _____
7) 24 _____ = 1 Day
8) ____ Minute = 60 Seconds
9) 12 Months = ____ Year
10) 60 Minutes = 1 _____
11) ____ Minute = 60 Seconds
12) 1 Minute = ____ Seconds
13) 24 _____ = 1 Day
14) 15 Minutes = ____ Hour
15) 365 Days = ____ Year
16) 365 Days = 1 _____
17) ____ Minutes = 1 Hour
18) 30 Minutes = 1/2 _____
19) ____ Weeks = 1 Year
20) ____ Minute = 60 Seconds

1) 15 Minutes = 1 _____
2) 12 _____ = 1 Year
3) 52 Weeks = ____ Year
4) 60 Seconds = ____ Minute
5) 12 Months = ____ Year
6) 1 _____ = 60 Seconds
7) 15 Minutes = ____ Hour
8) 52 Weeks = ____ Year
9) 15 _____ = 1/4 Hour
10) ____ Days = 1 Week
11) 1 Minute = 60 _____
12) ____ Days = 1 Year
13) 7 Days = ____ Week
14) ____ Minute = 60 Seconds
15) 52 Weeks = ____ Year
16) 1 Minute = ____ Seconds
17) 15 _____ = 1/4 Hour
18) ____ Weeks = 1 Year
19) ____ Minute = 60 Seconds
20) ____ Minutes = 1/2 Hour

Name: _____ Date: _____

PAGE 87

1) 12 Months = 1 _____
2) 24 Hours = 1 _____
3) 52 _____ = 1 Year
4) 365 Days = 1 _____
5) 52 Weeks = ____ Year
6) 7 Days = ____ Week
7) 7 Days = 1 _____
8) _____ Minutes = 1/2 Hour
9) _____ Minutes = 1/2 Hour
10) _____ Minutes = 1/2 Hour
11) _____ Months = 1 Year
12) _____ Weeks = 1 Year
13) 60 Minutes = 1 _____
14) 7 _____ = 1 Week
15) 1 Minute = ____ Seconds
16) 12 Months = ____ Year
17) 24 Hours = ____ Day
18) 365 Days = 1 _____
19) 15 Minutes = 1 _____
20) 12 Months = ____ Year

1) 52 Weeks = 1 _____
2) 7 Days = ____ Week
3) _____ Minute = 60 Seconds
4) 365 Days = ____ Year
5) 60 _____ = 1 Hour
6) 24 _____ = 1 Day
7) _____ Hours = 1 Day
8) 7 _____ = 1 Week
9) 60 _____ = 1 Hour
10) 24 Hours = 1 _____
11) 30 _____ = 1/2 Hour
12) _____ Minutes = 1/4 Hour
13) _____ Minute = 60 Seconds
14) 60 Minutes = ____ Hour
15) 60 Minutes = ____ Hour
16) 30 Minutes = ____ Hour
17) 24 _____ = 1 Day
18) 60 Seconds = 1 _____
19) _____ Seconds = 1 Minute
20) 15 Minutes = ____ Hour

Name: _____ Date: _____

PAGE 88

1) _____ Days = 1 Year
2) _____ Seconds = 1 Minute
3) 60 Seconds = _____ Minute
4) 24 Hours = 1 _____
5) _____ Days = 1 Week
6) 15 Minutes = 1 _____
7) _____ Minutes = 1 Hour
8) _____ Hours = 1 Day
9) _____ Minute = 60 Seconds
10) 60 Seconds = 1 _____
11) 60 _____ = 1 Hour
12) 60 _____ = 1 Minute
13) 7 _____ = 1 Week
14) 1 Minute = _____ Seconds
15) _____ Days = 1 Year
16) _____ Months = 1 Year
17) _____ Weeks = 1 Year
18) 52 _____ = 1 Year
19) 24 Hours = _____ Day
20) 1 _____ = 60 Seconds

1) _____ Days = 1 Year
2) 7 Days = _____ Week
3) 60 Minutes = _____ Hour
4) _____ Months = 1 Year
5) _____ Days = 1 Year
6) 12 Months = _____ Year
7) 60 Seconds = 1 _____
8) 12 Months = _____ Year
9) 365 _____ = 1 Year
10) 7 _____ = 1 Week
11) 1 _____ = 60 Seconds
12) _____ Seconds = 1 Minute
13) _____ Months = 1 Year
14) 15 Minutes = _____ Hour
15) 15 Minutes = 1 _____
16) 60 Minutes = _____ Hour
17) 365 Days = 1 _____
18) 15 _____ = 1/4 Hour
19) 365 _____ = 1 Year
20) _____ Minutes = 1/2 Hour

Name: _____ Date: _____

PAGE 89

Elapsed Days, Weeks, Months and Years

1) Sam was born on November 2, 1985. How old will he be on his
   birthday in 2017? _____

2) Jessica will arrive at the hotel on July 6th, and will stay four nights.
   What date will Jessica check out of the hotel? _____

3) Benny's vacation is from August 5th to August 21st. Tom's vacation starts on
   August 7th and lasts two weeks. Whose vacation is longer and by
   how many days? _____

4) Melanie's appointment with the dentist was on March 4th. The dentist wants to
see Melanie in three months. In what month should Melanie make an appointment? _____

5) Fred was 36 years old on September 4, 1997. In what year was he born?
   How old will he on September 4, 2015? _____

6) Many airlines make you purchase a ticket 14 days before your flight.
If Mary is leaving on December 20th, on what day should she purchase her ticket? _____

7) Keith was five years old on April 3rd. Joan was five years old on
   April 18th. How many days older is Keith? _____

8) The Pierce's left on a three-week vacation on June 5th. When did they return? _____

9) How many months, weeks, and days are there between May 7, 2018
   and August 22, 2018? _____

10) Nancy was born on May 3rd. Mary was born on October 3rd of the
    same year. How many months older is Nancy? _____

Name: _____   Date: _____

PAGE 90

Elapsed Days, Weeks, Months and Years

1) Benny will arrive at the hotel on July 8th, and will stay five nights.
   What date will Benny check out of the hotel?   _____

2) Many airlines make you purchase a ticket 14 days before your flight.
   If Sam is leaving on February 26th, on what day should he purchase his ticket ? _____

3) Dan's appointment with the dentist was on April 4th. The dentist wants to
   see Dan in six months. In what month should Dan make an appointment ?   _____

4) Fred's vacation is from October 6th to October 25th. Joan's vacation starts on
   October 7th and lasts two weeks. Whose vacation is longer and by
   how many days ?   _____

5) How many months, weeks, and days are there between May 3, 2012
   and December 18, 2012 ?   _____

6) The Matson's left on a three-week vacation on August 1st. When did they return ? _____

7) Jason was 34 years old on November 25, 1982. In what year was he born ?
   How old will he on November 25, 1994 ?   _____

8) Sara was nine years old on April 5th. Melanie was nine years old on
   April 23rd. How many days older is Sara ?   _____

9) Tom was born on January 15th. Sam was born on May 15th of the
   same year. How many months older is Tom ?   _____

10) Nancy was born on September 14, 1968. How old will she be on her
    birthday in 2013 ?   _____

Elapsed Days, Weeks, Months and Years

1) Tim was born on August 5th. Keith was born on September 5th of the same year. How many months older is Tim? _____

2) Mary was 37 years old on October 23, 1989. In what year was she born? How old will she be on October 23, 1999? _____

3) Jason was born on May 4, 1982. How old will he be on his birthday in 2013? _____

4) How many months, weeks, and days are there between May 12, 2015 and December 7, 2015? _____

5) The Pierce's left on a three-week vacation on April 5th. When did they return? _____

6) Sam was six years old on June 9th. Melanie was six years old on June 25th. How many days older is Sam? _____

7) Many airlines make you purchase a ticket 14 days before your flight. If Keith is leaving on December 21st, on what day should he purchase his ticket? _____

8) Dan's appointment with the doctor was on May 6th. The doctor wants to see Dan in five months. In what month should Dan make an appointment? _____

9) Jessica will arrive at the hotel on March 4th, and will stay three nights. What date will Jessica check out of the hotel? _____

10) Tom's vacation is from January 6th to January 17th. Sara's vacation starts on January 8th and lasts two weeks. Whose vacation is longer and by how many days? _____

Name: _____ Date: _____

PAGE 92

Elapsed Days, Weeks, Months and Years

1) How many months, weeks, and days are there between May 2, 2020 and August 18, 2020 ? _____

2) The Thompson's left on a three-week vacation on February 1st. When did they return ? _____

3) Sally will arrive at the hotel on September 2nd, and will stay three nights. What date will Sally check out of the hotel? _____

4) Tim was 30 years old on November 13, 1976. In what year was he born ? How old will he on November 13, 1995 ? _____

5) Many airlines make you purchase a ticket 14 days before your flight. If Keith is leaving on October 26th, on what day should he purchase his ticket ? _____

6) Mike's appointment with the doctor was on June 6th. The doctor wants to see Mike in two months. In what month should Mike make an appointment ? _____

7) Melanie's vacation is from July 6th to July 22nd. Fred's vacation starts on July 9th and lasts two weeks. Whose vacation is longer and by how many days ? _____

8) Sara was two years old on June 5th. Jason was two years old on June 20th. How many days older is Sara ? _____

9) Jessica was born on January 19, 1983. How old will she be on her birthday in 2012 ? _____

10) Joan was born on April 20th. Keith was born on May 20th of the same year. How many months older is Joan ? _____

Name: _____ Date: _____

PAGE 93

Elapsed Days, Weeks, Months and Years

1) Tim was born on April 14th. Benny was born on July 14th of the
    same year. How many months older is Tim ?   _____

2) Nancy was two years old on February 7th. Mary was two years old on
    February 26th. How many days older is Nancy ?   _____

3) Mike's vacation is from November 5th to November 15th. Tom's vacation starts on
    November 6th and lasts two weeks. Whose vacation is longer and by
    how many days ?   _____

4) Melanie was born on September 13, 1982. How old will she be on her
    birthday in 2017 ?   _____

5) Sara will arrive at the hotel on August 3rd, and will stay three nights.
    What date will Sara check out of the hotel?   _____

6) Sally was 23 years old on December 1, 1977. In what year was she born ?
    How old will she be on December 1, 1996 ?   _____

7) Jason's appointment with the doctor was on June 2nd. The doctor wants to
    see Jason in two months. In what month should Jason make an appointment ?   _____

8) How many months, weeks, and days are there between April 24, 2015
    and November 16, 2015 ?   _____

9) Many airlines make you purchase a ticket 14 days before your flight.
    If Benny is leaving on May 25th, on what day should he purchase his ticket ? _____

10) The Matson's left on a two-week vacation on March 3rd. When did they return ?

    _____

Elapsed Days, Weeks, Months and Years

1) Sam's appointment with the dentist was on June 10th. The dentist wants to see Sam in five months. In what month should Sam make an appointment?

2) Many airlines make you purchase a ticket 14 days before your flight. If Melanie is leaving on September 26th, on what day should she purchase her ticket?

   October 23rd. How many days older is Jason?
3) Jason was four years old on October 6th. Jessica was four years old on
4) The Hoffman's left on a three-week vacation on July 5th. When did they return?

5) Nancy was born on January 15, 1999. How old will she be on her birthday in 2012?

6) Sara was born on February 16th. Melanie was born on April 16th of the same year. How many months older is Sara?

7) Tim's vacation is from March 7th to March 23rd. Fred's vacation starts on March 8th and lasts two weeks. Whose vacation is longer and by how many days?

8) How many months, weeks, and days are there between May 5, 2018 and December 23, 2018?

9) Keith was 12 years old on December 9, 1991. In what year was he born? How old will he on December 9, 2010?

10) Dan will arrive at the hotel on November 7th, and will stay four nights. What date will Dan check out of the hotel?

Name: _____ Date: _____

PAGE 95

Elapsed Days, Weeks, Months and Years

1) Jason was 22 years old on July 14, 1994. In what year was he born?
   How old will he on July 14, 2005? _____

2) Many airlines make you purchase a ticket 14 days before your flight.
   If Sara is leaving on September 20th, on what day should she purchase her ticket? _____

3) Joan's appointment with the doctor was on February 11th. The doctor wants to
   see Joan in three months. In what month should Joan make an appointment? _____

4) Sally was born on April 15, 1990. How old will she be on her
   birthday in 2017? _____

5) Mary's vacation is from May 2nd to May 12th. Tim's vacation starts on
   May 4th and lasts two weeks. Whose vacation is longer and by
   how many days? _____

6) Nancy will arrive at the hotel on August 1st, and will stay five nights.
   What date will Nancy check out of the hotel? _____

7) How many months, weeks, and days are there between April 9, 2014
   and August 19, 2014? _____

8) Fred was seven years old on November 5th. Dan was seven years old on
   November 15th. How many days older is Fred? _____

9) The Perry's left on a one-week vacation on January 4th. When did they return? _____

10) Tom was born on June 16th. Sara was born on October 16th of the
    same year. How many months older is Tom? _____

Name: _____ Date: _____

PAGE 96

Elapsed Days, Weeks, Months and Years

1) The Perry's left on a one-week vacation on February 2nd. When did they return? _____

2) Benny was born on April 25, 1965. How old will he be on his birthday in 2016? _____

3) Fred was nine years old on June 3rd. Dan was nine years old on June 15th. How many days older is Fred? _____

4) Tim will arrive at the hotel on September 2nd, and will stay two nights. What date will Tim check out of the hotel? _____

5) How many months, weeks, and days are there between April 15, 2017 and November 1, 2017? _____

6) Sally's vacation is from August 10th to August 26th. Jason's vacation starts on August 13th and lasts two weeks. Whose vacation is longer and by how many days? _____

7) Many airlines make you purchase a ticket 14 days before your flight. If Sam is leaving on July 16th, on what day should he purchase his ticket? _____

8) Joan's appointment with the doctor was on June 6th. The doctor wants to see Joan in five months. In what month should Joan make an appointment? _____

9) Mary was born on January 26th. Sam was born on May 26th of the same year. How many months older is Mary? _____

10) Jessica was 30 years old on March 13, 1994. In what year was she born? How old will she be on March 13, 2012? _____

Name: _____ Date: _____

PAGE 97

Elapsed Days, Weeks, Months and Years

1) Fred was five years old on April 2nd. Jessica was five years old on
April 19th. How many days older is Fred ? _____

2) Tom will arrive at the hotel on February 12th, and will stay three nights.
What date will Tom check out of the hotel? _____

3) Joan was born on July 21st. Keith was born on September 21st of the
same year. How many months older is Joan ? _____

4) Melanie's vacation is from August 9th to August 20th. Tim's vacation starts on
August 12th and lasts two weeks. Whose vacation is longer and by
how many days ? _____

5) The Kennedy's left on a one-week vacation on December 3rd. When did they return ? _____

6) Dan was 25 years old on March 26, 1976. In what year was he born ?
How old will he on March 26, 1988 ? _____

7) Mike was born on May 20, 1980 . How old will he be on his
birthday in 2016 ? _____

8) Many airlines make you purchase a ticket 14 days before your flight.
If Keith is leaving on October 20th, on what day should he purchase his ticket ? _____

9) Sally's appointment with the dentist was on June 4th. The dentist wants to
see Sally in six months. In what month should Sally make an appointment ? _____

10) How many months, weeks, and days are there between March 17, 2019
and November 7, 2019 ? _____

Elapsed Days, Weeks, Months and Years

1) Sally was born on May 11, 1982. How old will she be on her birthday in 2017 ?

2) Mike was 30 years old on June 2, 1985. In what year was he born ? How old will he on June 2, 2003 ?

3) How many months, weeks, and days are there between March 1, 2018 and December 9, 2018 ?

4) The Matson's left on a one-week vacation on February 4th. When did they return ?

5) Tom's appointment with the dentist was on March 12th. The dentist wants to see Tom in three months. In what month should Tom make an appointment ?

6) Jason's vacation is from October 4th to October 23rd. Keith's vacation starts on October 5th and lasts two weeks. Whose vacation is longer and by how many days ?

7) Melanie was born on January 12th. Jessica was born on March 12th of the same year. How many months older is Melanie ?

8) Sara was seven years old on December 11th. Nancy was seven years old on December 16th. How many days older is Sara ?

9) Mary will arrive at the hotel on November 2nd, and will stay five nights. What date will Mary check out of the hotel?

10) Many airlines make you purchase a ticket 14 days before your flight. If Jessica is leaving on July 18th, on what day should she purchase her ticket ?

PAGE 98

Elapsed Days, Weeks, Months and Years

1) Jason's appointment with the doctor was on May 11th. The doctor wants to
     see Jason in four months. In what month should Jason make an appointment ? _____

2) Many airlines make you purchase a ticket 14 days before your flight.
     If Sara is leaving on March 21st, on what day should she purchase her ticket ? _____

3) How many months, weeks, and days are there between June 9, 2017
     and October 13, 2017 ? _____

4) Melanie was eight years old on November 10th. Jessica was eight years old on
     November 16th. How many days older is Melanie ? _____

5) Nancy was born on February 20, 1970. How old will she be on her
     birthday in 2014 ? _____

6) Sam will arrive at the hotel on January 4th, and will stay two nights.
     What date will Sam check out of the hotel? _____

7) The Hall's left on a two-week vacation on April 2nd. When did they return ? _____

8) Tom's vacation is from May 7th to May 25th. Mike's vacation starts on
     May 9th and lasts two weeks. Whose vacation is longer and by
     how many days ? _____

9) Benny was born on June 21st. Sara was born on December 21st of the
     same year. How many months older is Benny ? _____

10) Mary was 29 years old on September 22, 1971. In what year was she born ?
     How old will she be on September 22, 1982 ? _____

PAGE 99

Name: _____ Date: _____

PAGE 100

Elapsed Days, Weeks, Months and Years

1) Fred was five years old on February 9th. Benny was five years old on
   February 19th. How many days older is Fred ? _____

2) Many airlines make you purchase a ticket 14 days before your flight.
   If Sara is leaving on October 26th, on what day should she purchase her ticket ? _____

3) Jason was 37 years old on July 3, 1991. In what year was he born ?
   How old will he on July 3, 2002 ? _____

4) Joan will arrive at the hotel on November 8th, and will stay five nights.
   What date will Joan check out of the hotel? _____

5) Sam was born on January 14th. Sara was born on December 14th of the
   same year. How many months older is Sam ? _____

6) The Perry's left on a three-week vacation on August 5th. When did they return ? _____

7) Jessica's vacation is from April 3rd to April 22nd. Melanie's vacation starts on
   April 5th and lasts two weeks. Whose vacation is longer and by
   how many days ? _____

8) Mary's appointment with the doctor was on March 2nd. The doctor wants to
   see Mary in two months. In what month should Mary make an appointment ? _____

9) Tim was born on May 13, 1989 . How old will he be on his
   birthday in 2012 ? _____

10) How many months, weeks, and days are there between March 22, 2017
    and November 25, 2017 ? _____

HELP US IMPROVE!

WE WANT YOUR FEEDBACK

πMath

pimathpublishing@gmail.com

www.amazon.com

ANSWER KEY

page1

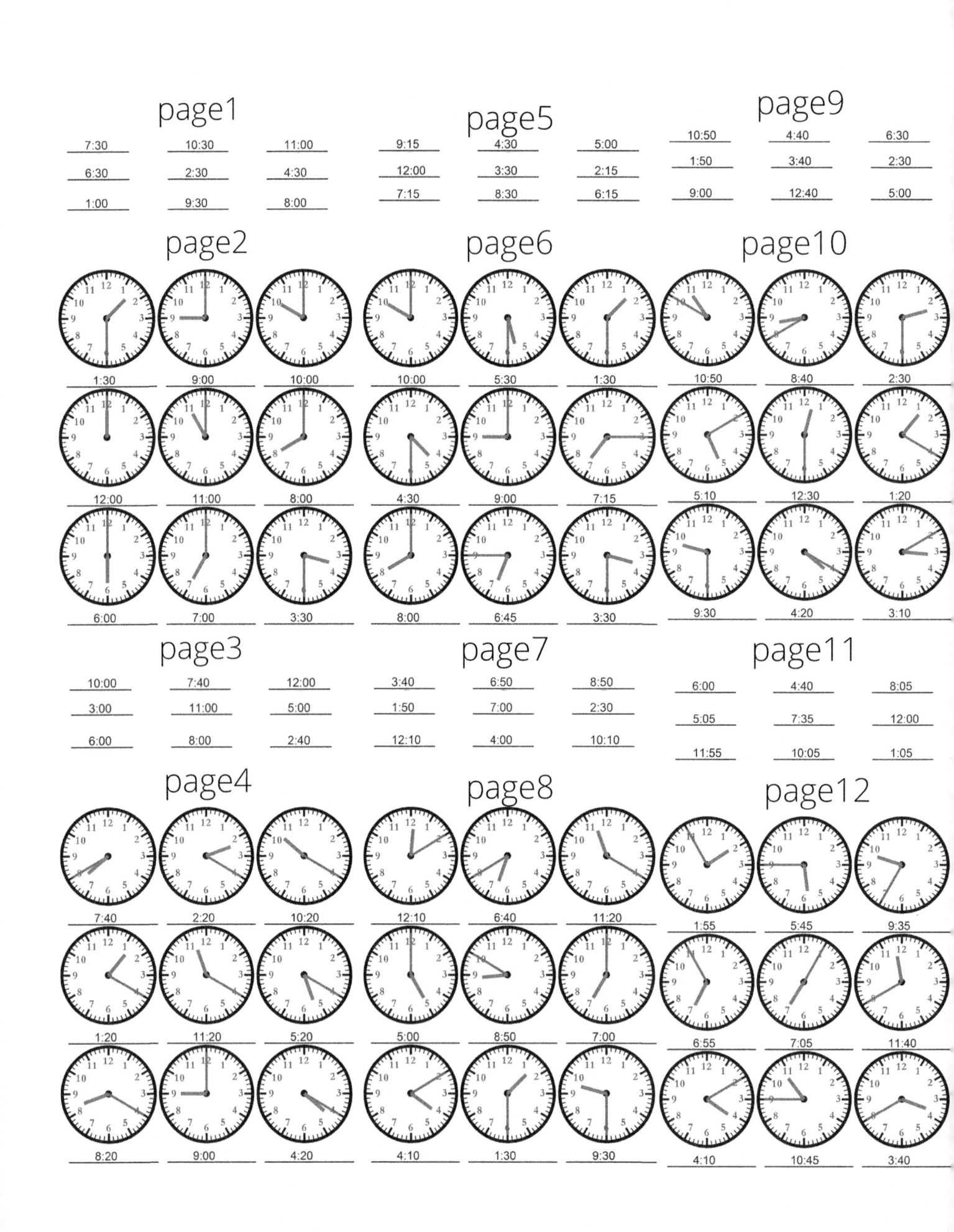

7:30   10:30   11:00

6:30   2:30   4:30

1:00   9:30   8:00

page2

1:30   9:00   10:00

12:00   11:00   8:00

6:00   7:00   3:30

page3

10:00   7:40   12:00

3:00   11:00   5:00

6:00   8:00   2:40

page4

7:40   2:20   10:20

1:20   11:20   5:20

8:20   9:00   4:20

page5

9:15   4:30   5:00

12:00   3:30   2:15

7:15   8:30   6:15

page6

10:00   5:30   1:30

4:30   9:00   7:15

8:00   6:45   3:30

page7

3:40   6:50   8:50

1:50   7:00   2:30

12:10   4:00   10:10

page8

12:10   6:40   11:20

5:00   8:50   7:00

4:10   1:30   9:30

page9

10:50   4:40   6:30

1:50   3:40   2:30

9:00   12:40   5:00

page10

10:50   8:40   2:30

5:10   12:30   1:20

9:30   4:20   3:10

page11

6:00   4:40   8:05

5:05   7:35   12:00

11:55   10:05   1:05

page12

1:55   5:45   9:35

6:55   7:05   11:40

4:10   10:45   3:40

page13

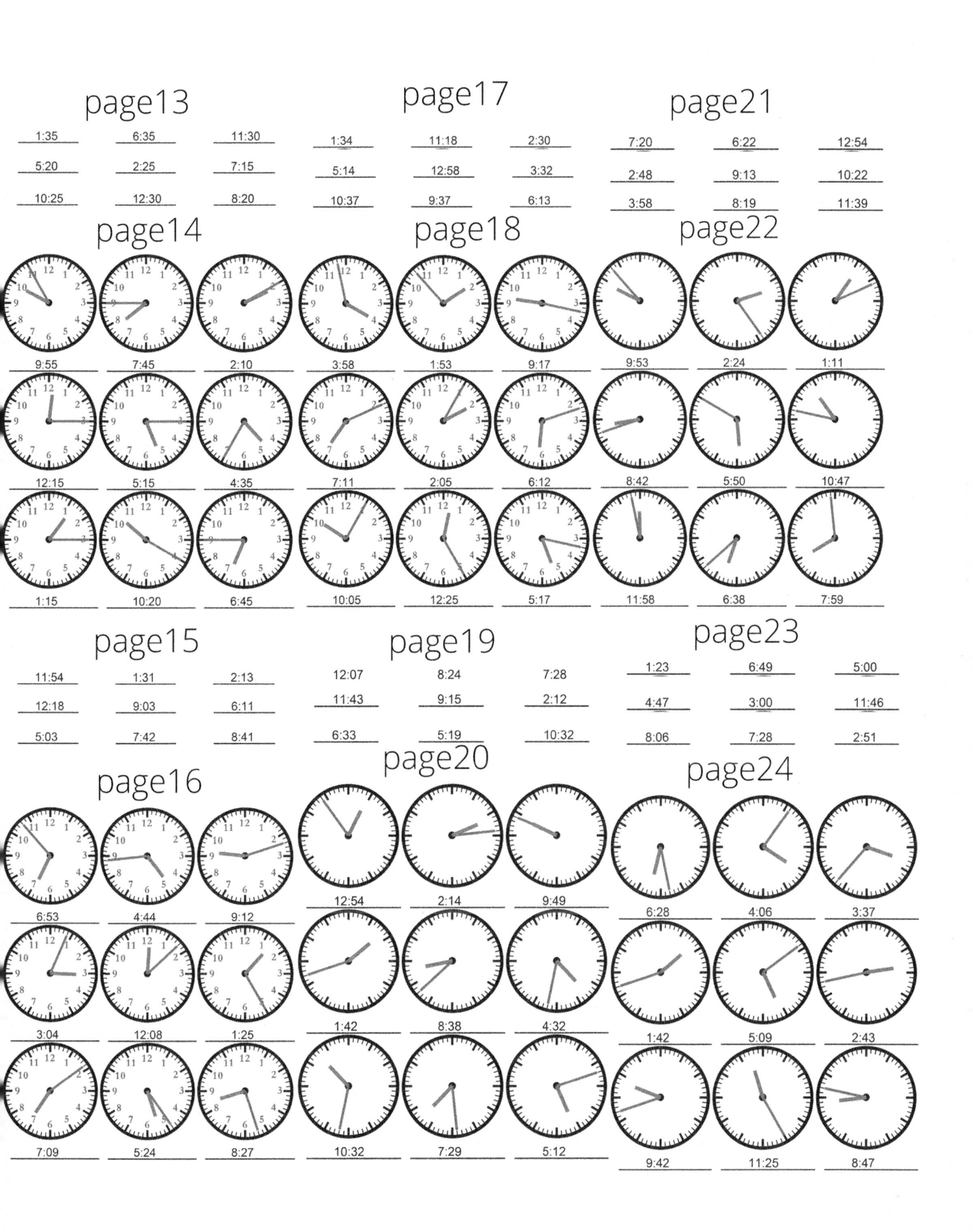

1:35	6:35	11:30
5:20	2:25	7:15
10:25	12:30	8:20

page14

9:55	7:45	2:10
12:15	5:15	4:35
1:15	10:20	6:45

page15

11:54	1:31	2:13
12:18	9:03	6:11
5:03	7:42	8:41

page16

6:53	4:44	9:12
3:04	12:08	1:25
7:09	5:24	8:27

page17

1:34	11:18	2:30
5:14	12:58	3:32
10:37	9:37	6:13

page18

3:58	1:53	9:17
7:11	2:05	6:12
10:05	12:25	5:17

page19

12:07	8:24	7:28
11:43	9:15	2:12
6:33	5:19	10:32

page20

12:54	2:14	9:49
1:42	8:38	4:32
10:32	7:29	5:12

page21

7:20	6:22	12:54
2:48	9:13	10:22
3:58	8:19	11:39

page22

9:53	2:24	1:11
8:42	5:50	10:47
11:58	6:38	7:59

page23

1:23	6:49	5:00
4:47	3:00	11:46
8:06	7:28	2:51

page24

6:28	4:06	3:37
1:42	5:09	2:43
9:42	11:25	8:47

page25

D. 3:30 PM
C. 8:30 PM
E. 5:15 AM
B. 10:45 PM
A. 2:15 PM

page26

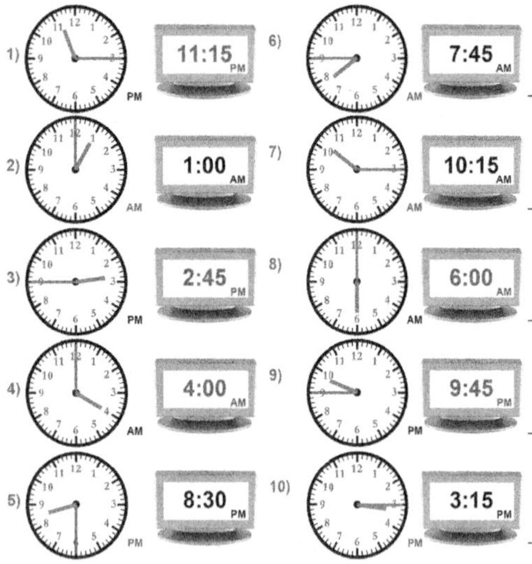

1) 11:15 PM
2) 1:00 AM
3) 2:45 PM
4) 4:00 AM
5) 8:30 PM
6) 7:45 AM
7) 10:15 AM
8) 6:00 AM
9) 9:45 PM
10) 3:15 PM

page31

B. 10:00 PM
E. 1:20 AM
D. 3:55 PM
A. 8:25 PM
C. 4:50 AM

page32

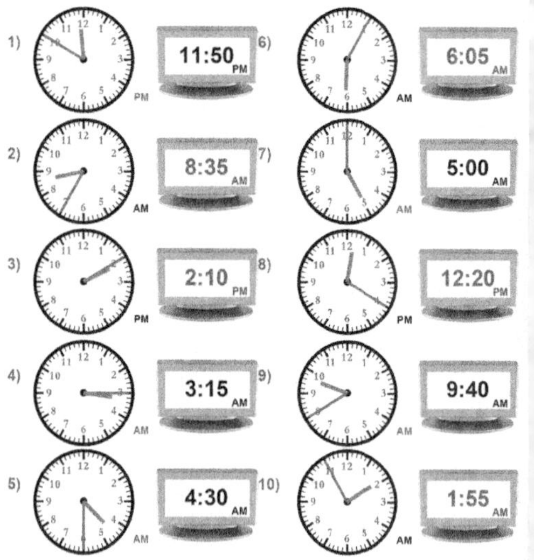

1) 11:50 PM
2) 8:35 AM
3) 2:10 PM
4) 3:15 AM
5) 4:30 AM
6) 6:05 AM
7) 5:00 AM
8) 12:20 PM
9) 9:40 AM
10) 1:55 AM

pag27

B. 9:30 AM
A. 8:00 AM
D. 11:20 PM
E. 7:40 PM
C. 2:50 PM

page28

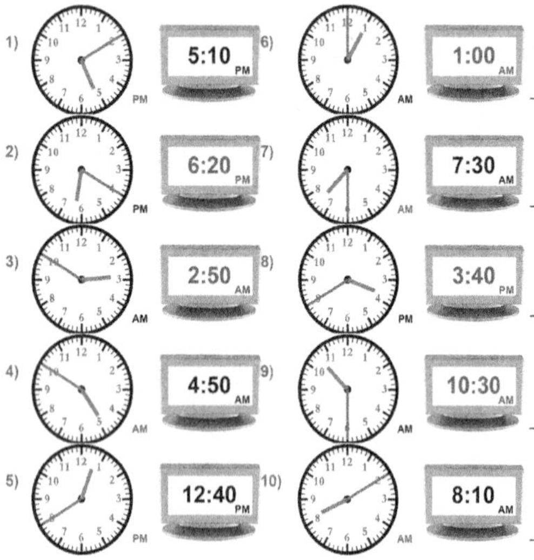

1) 5:10 PM
2) 6:20 PM
3) 2:50 AM
4) 4:50 AM
5) 12:40 PM
6) 1:00 AM
7) 7:30 AM
8) 3:40 PM
9) 10:30 AM
10) 8:10 AM

page33

B. 8:02 AM
E. 5:32 AM
D. 6:37 PM
A. 2:38 AM
C. 12:33 PM

page34

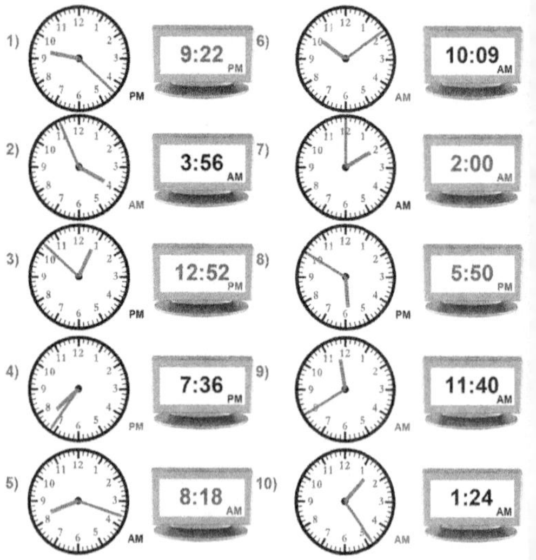

1) 9:22 PM
2) 3:56 AM
3) 12:52 PM
4) 7:36 PM
5) 8:18 AM
6) 10:09 AM
7) 2:00 AM
8) 5:50 PM
9) 11:40 AM
10) 1:24 AM

page29

B. 1:15 AM
C. 10:10 PM
E. 11:45 PM
A. 6:20 AM
D. 5:35 AM

page30

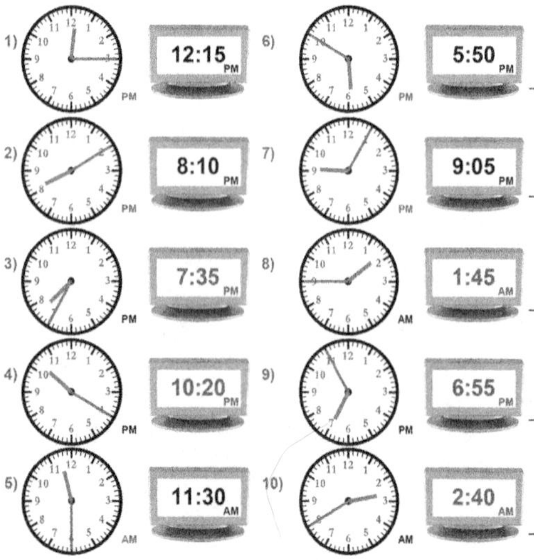

1) 12:15 PM
2) 8:10 PM
3) 7:35 PM
4) 10:20 PM
5) 11:30 AM
6) 5:50 PM
7) 9:05 PM
8) 1:45 AM
9) 6:55 PM
10) 2:40 AM

page35

D. 12:54 PM
E. 6:48 AM
C. 10:35 PM
A. 4:45 AM
B. 5:20 PM

page36

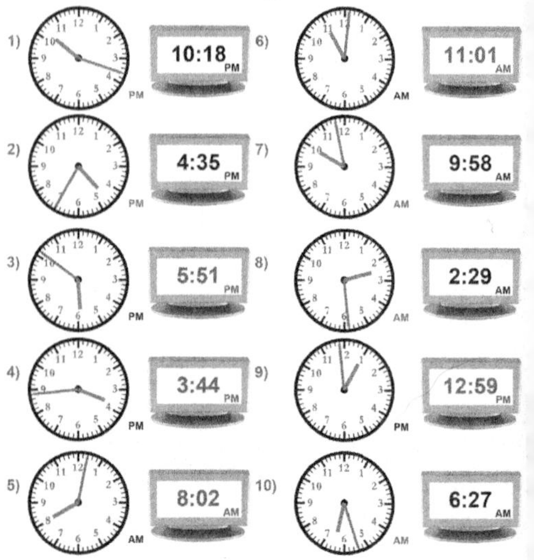

1) 10:18 PM
2) 4:35 PM
3) 5:51 PM
4) 3:44 PM
5) 8:02 AM
6) 11:01 AM
7) 9:58 AM
8) 2:29 AM
9) 12:59 PM
10) 6:27 AM

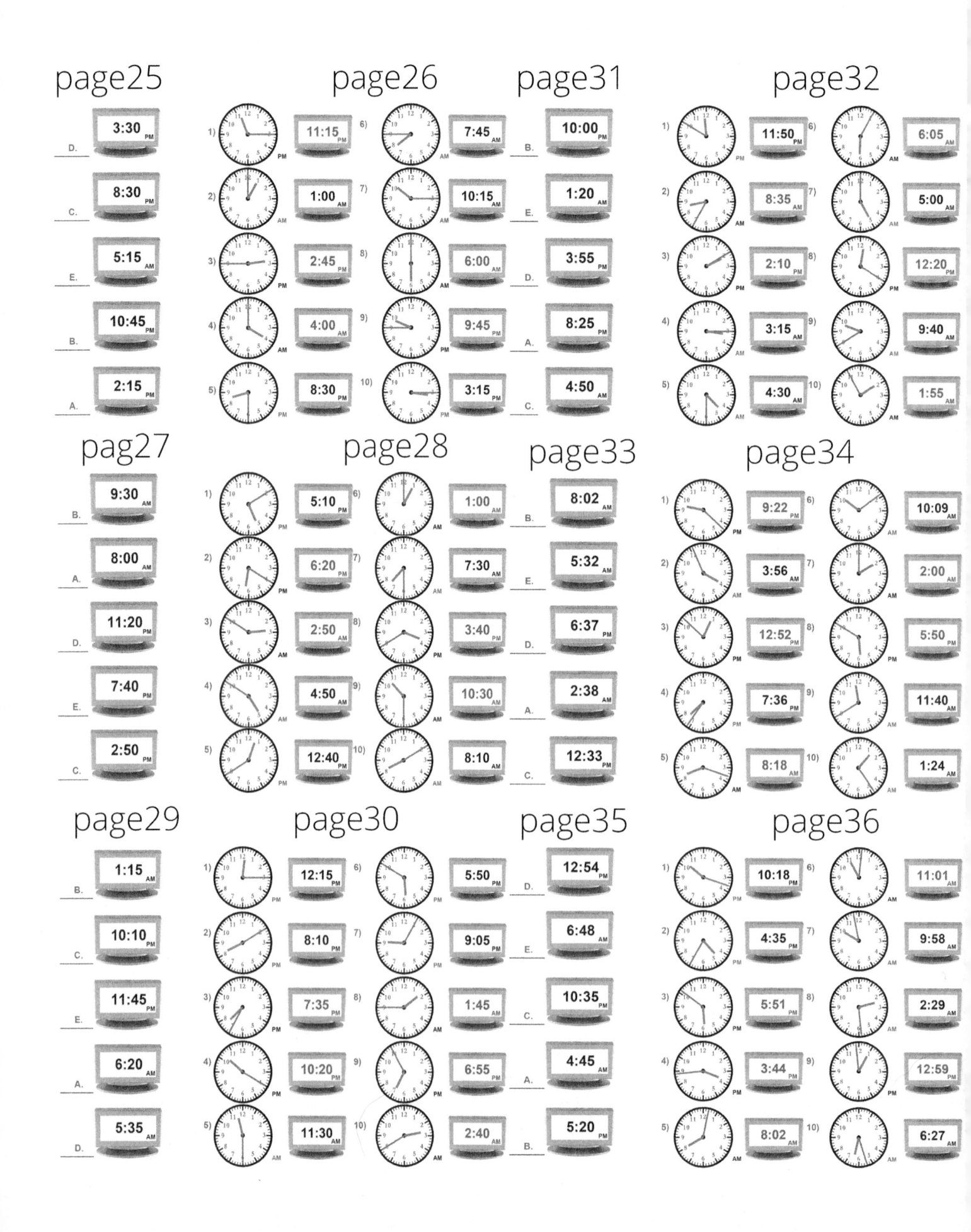

page41

6:05
10:05
5:05
8:05
4:30
1:30
12:30
6:30
9:00
5:00
10:00
7:00
3:40
5:40
2:40
11:40

page42

11:30
1:30
8:30
3:30
11:55
2:55
10:55
6:55
7:00
10:00
6:00
9:00
1:10
9:10
6:10
4:10

page43

6:30
4:30
8:00
6:00
7:05
5:35
7:35
9:05
9:25
10:25
7:25
9:55
2:20
3:50
4:20
1:50

page44

9:40
9:00
11:00
10:00
4:10
2:30
4:30
3:10
11:20
12:40
1:00
10:40
5:50
5:10
4:30
6:50

page45

11:05
10:50
11:35
12:35
9:40
8:10
9:10
10:55
7:50
8:35
7:20
6:35
4:25
4:55
2:55
3:25

page46

2:25
3:35
1:25
1:55
7:50
6:30
8:40
8:30
6:05
5:05
6:25
4:55
2:40
4:00
1:50
3:10

page47

7:15
6:25
8:00
6:40
5:00
6:00
5:45
4:25
6:10
5:20
5:40
6:50
12:20
1:00
12:50
11:25

page48

3:55
4:06
3:20
3:32
6:20
7:14
5:44
5:22
7:05
6:18
6:39
7:20
4:40
4:59
4:29
5:41

page49

10:30
7:00
9:00
2:30
11:45
9:45
1:15
3:15
8:15
11:45
5:45
7:15
12:05
4:05
2:35
9:05

page50

1:20
5:50
3:20
11:35
11:30
1:45
8:30
7:00
12:45
3:00
8:15
9:00
10:50
1:50
6:35
12:20

page51

10:09

1:08

3:48

1:39

11:45

6:14

8:03

6:50

3:48

8:15

5:33

10:01

6:31

4:15

3:58

10:10

page52

6:11

9:46

1:32

10:34

2:13

5:28

6:43

7:59

5:01

1:57

12:09

7:45

9:57

7:43

2:57

5:26

page53

8:30

9:30

1 hrs and 0 mins

11:30

8:30

9 hrs and 0 mins

1:00

9:00

8 hrs and 0 mins

3:30

8:30

5 hrs and 0 mins

page54

3 Hours & 0 Minutes

5 Hours & 0 Minutes

5 Hours & 0 Minutes

4 Hours & 0 Minutes

3 Hours & 0 Minutes

3 Hours & 0 Minutes

1 Hours & 0 Minutes

2 Hours & 0 Minutes

5 Hours & 0 Minutes

5 Hours & 0 Minutes

4 Hours & 0 Minutes

2 Hours & 0 Minutes

3 Hours & 0 Minutes

2 Hours & 0 Minutes

5 Hours & 0 Minutes

page55

4:30

4:39

0 hrs and 9 mins

2:30

2:35

0 hrs and 5 mins

6:30

6:31

0 hrs and 1 mins

12:30

12:33

0 hrs and 3 mins

page56

5 Hours & 0 Minutes

1 Hours & 0 Minutes

3 Hours & 0 Minutes

3 Hours & 0 Minutes

4 Hours & 0 Minutes

2 Hours & 0 Minutes

5 Hours & 0 Minutes

2 Hours & 0 Minutes

4 Hours & 0 Minutes

2 Hours & 0 Minutes

2 Hours & 0 Minutes

5 Hours & 0 Minutes

5 Hours & 0 Minutes

4 Hours & 0 Minutes

2 Hours & 0 Minutes

page57

6:00

6:13

0 hrs and 13 mins

12:30

12:38

0 hrs and 8 mins

5:30

5:44

0 hrs and 14 mins

7:30

7:43

0 hrs and 13 mins

page58

4 Hours & 0 Minutes

2 Hours & 0 Minutes

4 Hours & 0 Minutes

2 Hours & 0 Minutes

3 Hours & 0 Minutes

4 Hours & 0 Minutes

2 Hours & 0 Minutes

4 Hours & 0 Minutes

2 Hours & 0 Minutes

3 Hours & 0 Minutes

2 Hours & 0 Minutes

3 Hours & 0 Minutes

1 Hours & 0 Minutes

1 Hours & 0 Minutes

4 Hours & 0 Minutes

page59

9:15

9:29

0 hrs and 14 mins

1:30

1:47

0 hrs and 17 mins

1:15

1:33

0 hrs and 18 mins

7:15

7:26

0 hrs and 11 mins

page60

0 Hours & 21 Minutes

0 Hours & 59 Minutes

0 Hours & 50 Minutes

0 Hours & 41 Minutes

0 Hours & 16 Minutes

0 Hours & 49 Minutes

0 Hours & 54 Minutes

0 Hours & 36 Minutes

0 Hours & 32 Minutes

0 Hours & 44 Minutes

0 Hours & 35 Minutes

0 Hours & 15 Minutes

0 Hours & 28 Minutes

0 Hours & 21 Minutes

0 Hours & 53 Minutes

page61
9:15
9:38
0 hrs and 23 mins

1:10
1:34
0 hrs and 24 mins

4:20
4:43
0 hrs and 23 mins

4:30
4:53
0 hrs and 23 mins

page62
0 Hours & 35 Minutes
0 Hours & 13 Minutes
0 Hours & 16 Minutes
0 Hours & 37 Minutes
0 Hours & 11 Minutes
0 Hours & 33 Minutes
0 Hours & 25 Minutes
0 Hours & 37 Minutes
0 Hours & 57 Minutes
0 Hours & 34 Minutes
0 Hours & 42 Minutes
0 Hours & 38 Minutes
0 Hours & 45 Minutes
0 Hours & 39 Minutes
0 Hours & 39 Minutes

page63
4:05
4:34
0 hrs and 29 mins

1:20
1:42
0 hrs and 22 mins

8:10
8:31
0 hrs and 21 mins

10:30
10:53
0 hrs and 23 mins

page64
0 Hours & 27 Minutes
0 Hours & 55 Minutes
0 Hours & 58 Minutes
0 Hours & 34 Minutes
0 Hours & 19 Minutes
0 Hours & 22 Minutes
0 Hours & 53 Minutes
0 Hours & 32 Minutes
0 Hours & 43 Minutes
0 Hours & 46 Minutes
0 Hours & 39 Minutes
0 Hours & 18 Minutes
0 Hours & 45 Minutes
0 Hours & 16 Minutes
0 Hours & 55 Minutes

page65
5:20
11:14
5 hrs and 54 mins

3:40
9:48
6 hrs and 8 mins

9:40
11:20
1 hrs and 40 mins

5:20
11:56
6 hrs and 36 mins

page66
1 Hours & 55 Minutes
3 Hours & 53 Minutes
1 Hours & 11 Minutes
2 Hours & 54 Minutes
1 Hours & 29 Minutes
1 Hours & 57 Minutes
4 Hours & 45 Minutes
1 Hours & 51 Minutes
3 Hours & 56 Minutes
3 Hours & 48 Minutes
1 Hours & 11 Minutes
3 Hours & 18 Minutes
2 Hours & 30 Minutes
2 Hours & 51 Minutes
1 Hours & 31 Minutes

page67
8:55
1:59
5 hrs and 4 mins

12:55
4:02
3 hrs and 7 mins

7:20
10:36
3 hrs and 16 mins

2:30
10:38
8 hrs and 8 mins

page68
4 Hours & 39 Minutes
2 Hours & 23 Minutes
1 Hours & 29 Minutes
2 Hours & 43 Minutes
4 Hours & 48 Minutes
4 Hours & 58 Minutes
4 Hours & 37 Minutes
2 Hours & 33 Minutes
4 Hours & 12 Minutes
4 Hours & 54 Minutes
1 Hours & 12 Minutes
4 Hours & 50 Minutes
1 Hours & 30 Minutes
3 Hours & 39 Minutes
4 Hours & 49 Minutes

page69
What time is on Clock A? 6:05
What time is on Clock B? 11:08
How much time has elapsed between Clock A and B? 5 hrs and 3 mins

What time is on Clock A? 5:20
What time is on Clock B? 10:01
How much time has elapsed between Clock A and B? 4 hrs and 41 mins

What time is on Clock A? 4:50
What time is on Clock B? 10:32
How much time has elapsed between Clock A and B? 5 hrs and 42 mins

What time is on Clock A? 3:50
What time is on Clock B? 11:58
How much time has elapsed between Clock A and B? 8 hrs and 8 mins

page70
3 Hours & 11 Minutes
1 Hours & 10 Minutes
4 Hours & 59 Minutes
1 Hours & 46 Minutes
2 Hours & 45 Minutes
3 Hours & 35 Minutes
3 Hours & 11 Minutes
4 Hours & 29 Minutes
4 Hours & 50 Minutes
2 Hours & 26 Minutes
1 Hours & 21 Minutes
4 Hours & 33 Minutes
1 Hours & 37 Minutes
1 Hours & 39 Minutes
2 Hours & 51 Minutes

page71
4:50
10:45
5 hrs and 55 mins

3:40
5:19
1 hrs and 39 mins

7:05
11:35
4 hrs and 30 mins

5:25
2:57
9 hrs and 32 mins

page72
1 Hours & 19 Minutes
3 Hours & 27 Minutes
3 Hours & 18 Minutes
2 Hours & 52 Minutes
4 Hours & 11 Minutes
1 Hours & 18 Minutes
3 Hours & 35 Minutes
3 Hours & 15 Minutes
1 Hours & 30 Minutes
4 Hours & 27 Minutes
2 Hours & 11 Minutes
2 Hours & 56 Minutes
3 Hours & 44 Minutes
2 Hours & 45 Minutes
3 Hours & 28 Minutes

page73
8:27
9:40
1 hrs and 13 mins

3:36
6:47
3 hrs and 11 mins

6:17
8:21
2 hrs and 4 mins

1:43
2:03
0 hrs and 20 mins

page74
2 Hours & 45 Minutes
5 Hours & 49 Minutes
1 Hours & 29 Minutes
8 Hours & 46 Minutes
8 Hours & 17 Minutes
5 Hours & 55 Minutes
8 Hours & 36 Minutes
9 Hours & 52 Minutes
1 Hours & 41 Minutes
8 Hours & 46 Minutes
3 Hours & 43 Minutes
3 Hours & 43 Minutes
9 Hours & 47 Minutes
1 Hours & 25 Minutes
6 Hours & 38 Minutes

page75
6:03
9:53
3 hrs and 50 mins

12:46
8:59
8 hrs and 13 mins

7:33
3:53
8 hrs and 20 mins

5:40
3:55
10 hrs and 15 mins

page76
9 Hours & 13 Minutes
4 Hours & 31 Minutes
2 Hours & 19 Minutes
1 Hours & 56 Minutes
5 Hours & 52 Minutes
6 Hours & 52 Minutes
1 Hours & 51 Minutes
6 Hours & 41 Minutes
6 Hours & 16 Minutes
4 Hours & 45 Minutes
9 Hours & 10 Minutes
5 Hours & 52 Minutes
6 Hours & 19 Minutes
4 Hours & 20 Minutes
8 Hours & 40 Minutes

page77

Start Time	End Time	Elapsed Time
1:00 P.M.	4:00 P.M.	3 Hours & 0 Minutes
11:20 A.M.	12:20 P.M.	1 Hours & 0 Minutes
12:00 A.M.	5:00 A.M.	5 Hours & 0 Minutes
2:40 A.M.	3:40 A.M.	1 Hours & 0 Minutes
9:40 P.M.	11:40 P.M.	2 Hours & 0 Minutes
8:00 A.M.	9:00 A.M.	1 Hours & 0 Minutes
1:00 P.M.	6:00 P.M.	5 Hours & 0 Minutes
2:40 P.M.	6:40 P.M.	4 Hours & 0 Minutes
11:00 A.M.	4:00 P.M.	5 Hours & 0 Minutes
3:40 P.M.	7:40 P.M.	4 Hours & 0 Minutes

page78

Start Time	End Time	Elapsed Time
3:35 A.M.	4:35 A.M.	1 Hours & 0 Minutes
3:15 A.M.	7:15 A.M.	4 Hours & 0 Minutes
2:10 A.M.	4:10 A.M.	2 Hours & 0 Minutes
1:40 P.M.	5:40 P.M.	4 Hours & 0 Minutes
3:20 P.M.	5:20 P.M.	2 Hours & 0 Minutes
10:10 A.M.	11:10 A.M.	1 Hours & 0 Minutes
7:55 A.M.	12:55 P.M.	5 Hours & 0 Minutes
6:50 P.M.	9:50 P.M.	3 Hours & 0 Minutes
10:40 A.M.	11:40 A.M.	1 Hours & 0 Minutes
10:10 A.M.	3:10 P.M.	5 Hours & 0 Minutes

page79

Start Time	End Time	Elapsed Time
5:05 A.M.	5:26 A.M.	0 Hours & 21 Minutes
5:25 A.M.	6:06 A.M.	0 Hours & 41 Minutes
8:05 A.M.	8:17 A.M.	0 Hours & 12 Minutes
3:40 P.M.	4:26 P.M.	0 Hours & 46 Minutes
3:15 P.M.	3:41 P.M.	0 Hours & 26 Minutes
5:05 P.M.	5:21 P.M.	0 Hours & 16 Minutes
3:15 P.M.	3:37 P.M.	0 Hours & 22 Minutes
8:45 P.M.	9:21 P.M.	0 Hours & 36 Minutes
12:35 A.M.	12:51 A.M.	0 Hours & 16 Minutes
3:05 A.M.	3:37 A.M.	0 Hours & 32 Minutes

page80

Start Time	End Time	Elapsed Time
7:25 P.M.	8:01 P.M.	0 Hours & 36 Minutes
8:05 P.M.	8:34 P.M.	0 Hours & 29 Minutes
1:50 P.M.	2:42 P.M.	0 Hours & 52 Minutes
3:45 P.M.	4:00 P.M.	0 Hours & 15 Minutes
12:50 A.M.	1:18 A.M.	0 Hours & 28 Minutes
4:50 A.M.	5:19 A.M.	0 Hours & 29 Minutes
7:00 A.M.	7:39 A.M.	0 Hours & 39 Minutes
4:20 P.M.	4:37 P.M.	0 Hours & 17 Minutes
8:20 A.M.	9:19 A.M.	0 Hours & 59 Minutes
6:15 P.M.	7:00 P.M.	0 Hours & 45 Minutes

page81

Start Time	End Time	Elapsed Time
4:40 P.M.	7:26 P.M.	2 Hours & 46 Minutes
3:10 P.M.	8:03 P.M.	4 Hours & 53 Minutes
4:55 A.M.	7:36 A.M.	2 Hours & 41 Minutes
10:55 A.M.	3:10 P.M.	4 Hours & 15 Minutes
4:15 A.M.	9:06 A.M.	4 Hours & 51 Minutes
3:00 P.M.	7:23 P.M.	4 Hours & 23 Minutes
10:35 P.M.	1:18 A.M.	2 Hours & 43 Minutes
7:10 P.M.	9:03 P.M.	1 Hours & 53 Minutes
9:40 A.M.	12:54 P.M.	3 Hours & 14 Minutes
2:35 P.M.	7:03 P.M.	4 Hours & 28 Minutes

page82

Start Time	End Time	Elapsed Time
8:15 P.M.	12:01 A.M.	3 Hours & 46 Minutes
4:25 A.M.	7:22 A.M.	2 Hours & 57 Minutes
8:30 A.M.	11:47 A.M.	3 Hours & 17 Minutes
8:30 A.M.	1:07 P.M.	4 Hours & 37 Minutes
3:55 P.M.	5:32 P.M.	1 Hours & 37 Minutes
9:40 P.M.	12:10 A.M.	2 Hours & 30 Minutes
7:55 A.M.	12:54 P.M.	4 Hours & 59 Minutes
4:10 A.M.	7:28 A.M.	3 Hours & 18 Minutes
1:20 P.M.	3:53 P.M.	2 Hours & 33 Minutes
7:40 P.M.	11:04 P.M.	3 Hours & 24 Minutes

page83

Start Time	End Time	Elapsed Time
4:05 P.M.	8:02 P.M.	3 Hours & 57 Minutes
8:10 A.M.	12:32 P.M.	4 Hours & 22 Minutes
11:05 P.M.	12:26 A.M.	1 Hours & 21 Minutes
8:25 A.M.	11:59 A.M.	3 Hours & 34 Minutes
2:30 A.M.	5:40 A.M.	3 Hours & 10 Minutes
12:30 P.M.	2:45 P.M.	2 Hours & 15 Minutes
3:15 A.M.	5:32 A.M.	2 Hours & 17 Minutes
1:30 A.M.	5:07 A.M.	3 Hours & 37 Minutes
3:20 A.M.	6:48 A.M.	3 Hours & 28 Minutes
12:45 A.M.	2:01 A.M.	1 Hours & 16 Minutes

page84

Start Time	End Time	Elapsed Time
1:45 A.M.	5:00 A.M.	3 Hours & 15 Minutes
11:20 A.M.	3:04 P.M.	3 Hours & 44 Minutes
7:55 P.M.	10:53 P.M.	2 Hours & 58 Minutes
1:50 A.M.	4:21 A.M.	2 Hours & 31 Minutes
4:35 A.M.	5:55 A.M.	1 Hours & 20 Minutes
2:00 A.M.	4:12 A.M.	2 Hours & 12 Minutes
9:50 A.M.	2:39 P.M.	4 Hours & 49 Minutes
1:05 A.M.	3:00 A.M.	1 Hours & 55 Minutes
11:00 P.M.	3:57 A.M.	4 Hours & 57 Minutes
3:25 P.M.	4:48 P.M.	1 Hours & 23 Minutes

page85

1) 60 Seconds = 1 Minute
2) 30 Minutes = 1/2 Hour
3) 60 Minutes = 1 Hour
4) 365 Days = 1 Year
5) 365 Days = 1 Year
6) 15 Minutes = 1/4 Hour
7) 60 Minutes = 1 Hour
8) 12 Months = 1 Year
9) 7 Days = 1 Week
10) 365 Days = 1 Year
11) 1 Minute = 60 Seconds
12) 1 Minute = 60 Seconds
13) 60 Minutes = 1 Hour
14) 15 Minutes = 1/4 Hour
15) 365 Days = 1 Year
16) 52 Weeks = 1 Year
17) 24 Hours = 1 Day
18) 30 Minutes = 1/2 Hour
19) 1 Minute = 60 Seconds
20) 1 Minute = 60 Seconds

1) 30 Minutes = 1/2 Hour
2) 12 Months = 1 Year
3) 60 Seconds = 1 Minute
4) 52 Weeks = 1 Year
5) 60 Seconds = 1 Minute
6) 60 Minutes = 1 Hour
7) 1 Minute = 60 Seconds
8) 60 Minutes = 1 Hour
9) 7 Days = 1 Week
10) 7 Days = 1 Week
11) 52 Weeks = 1 Year
12) 15 Minutes = 1/4 Hour
13) 365 Days = 1 Year
14) 15 Minutes = 1/4 Hour
15) 24 Hours = 1 Day
16) 60 Seconds = 1 Minute
17) 15 Minutes = 1/4 Hour
18) 60 Minutes = 1 Hour
19) 24 Hours = 1 Day
20) 60 Minutes = 1 Hour

page86

1) 60 Minutes = 1 Hour
2) 7 Days = 1 Week
3) 7 Days = 1 Week
4) 12 Months = 1 Year
5) 12 Months = 1 Year
6) 12 Months = 1 Year
7) 24 Hours = 1 Day
8) 1 Minute = 60 Seconds
9) 12 Months = 1 Year
10) 60 Minutes = 1 Hour
11) 1 Minute = 60 Seconds
12) 1 Minute = 60 Seconds
13) 24 Hours = 1 Day
14) 15 Minutes = 1/4 Hour
15) 365 Days = 1 Year
16) 365 Days = 1 Year
17) 60 Minutes = 1 Hour
18) 30 Minutes = 1/2 Hour
19) 52 Weeks = 1 Year
20) 1 Minute = 60 Seconds

1) 15 Minutes = 1/4 Hour
2) 12 Months = 1 Year
3) 52 Weeks = 1 Year
4) 60 Seconds = 1 Minute
5) 12 Months = 1 Year
6) 1 Minute = 60 Seconds
7) 15 Minutes = 1/4 Hour
8) 52 Weeks = 1 Year
9) 15 Minutes = 1/4 Hour
10) 7 Days = 1 Week
11) 1 Minute = 60 Seconds
12) 365 Days = 1 Year
13) 7 Days = 1 Week
14) 1 Minute = 60 Seconds
15) 52 Weeks = 1 Year
16) 1 Minute = 60 Seconds
17) 15 Minutes = 1/4 Hour
18) 52 Weeks = 1 Year
19) 1 Minute = 60 Seconds
20) 30 Minutes = 1/2 Hour

page87

1) 12 Months = 1 Year
2) 24 Hours = 1 Day
3) 52 Weeks = 1 Year
4) 365 Days = 1 Year
5) 52 Weeks = 1 Year
6) 7 Days = 1 Week
7) 7 Days = 1 Week
8) 30 Minutes = 1/2 Hour
9) 30 Minutes = 1/2 Hour
10) 30 Minutes = 1/2 Hour
11) 12 Months = 1 Year
12) 52 Weeks = 1 Year
13) 60 Minutes = 1 Hour
14) 7 Days = 1 Week
15) 1 Minute = 60 Seconds
16) 12 Months = 1 Year
17) 24 Hours = 1 Day
18) 365 Days = 1 Year
19) 15 Minutes = 1/4 Hour
20) 12 Months = 1 Year

1) 52 Weeks = 1 Year
2) 7 Days = 1 Week
3) 1 Minute = 60 Seconds
4) 365 Days = 1 Year
5) 60 Minutes = 1 Hour
6) 24 Hours = 1 Day
7) 24 Hours = 1 Day
8) 7 Days = 1 Week
9) 24 Hours = 1 Day
10) 24 Hours = 1 Day
11) 30 Minutes = 1/2 Hour
12) 15 Minutes = 1/4 Hour
13) 1 Minute = 60 Seconds
14) 60 Minutes = 1 Hour
15) 60 Minutes = 1 Hour
16) 30 Minutes = 1/2 Hour
17) 24 Hours = 1 Day
18) 60 Seconds = 1 Minute
19) 60 Seconds = 1 Minute
20) 15 Minutes = 1/4 Hour

page88

1) 365 Days = 1 Year
2) 60 Seconds = 1 Minute
3) 60 Seconds = 1 Minute
4) 24 Hours = 1 Day
5) 7 Days = 1 Week
6) 15 Minutes = 1/4 Hour
7) 60 Minutes = 1 Hour
8) 24 Hours = 1 Day
9) 1 Minute = 60 Seconds
10) 60 Seconds = 1 Minute
11) 60 Minutes = 1 Hour
12) 60 Seconds = 1 Minute
13) 7 Days = 1 Week
14) 1 Minute = 60 Seconds
15) 365 Days = 1 Year
16) 12 Months = 1 Year
17) 52 Weeks = 1 Year
18) 52 Weeks = 1 Year
19) 24 Hours = 1 Day
20) 1 Minute = 60 Seconds

1) 365 Days = 1 Year
2) 7 Days = 1 Week
3) 60 Minutes = 1 Hour
4) 12 Months = 1 Year
5) 365 Days = 1 Year
6) 12 Months = 1 Year
7) 60 Seconds = 1 Minute
8) 12 Months = 1 Year
9) 365 Days = 1 Year
10) 7 Days = 1 Week
11) 1 Minute = 60 Seconds
12) 60 Seconds = 1 Minute
13) 12 Months = 1 Year
14) 15 Minutes = 1/4 Hour
15) 15 Minutes = 1/4 Hour
16) 60 Minutes = 1 Hour
17) 365 Days = 1 Year
18) 15 Minutes = 1/4 Hour
19) 365 Days = 1 Year
20) 30 Minutes = 1/2 Hour

page89

32 years

July 10th

Benny's by 2 days

June

1961 | 54

December 6th

15 days

June 26th

3 months, 2 weeks, & 1 day

5 months

page90

July 13th

February 12th

October

Fred's by 5 days

7 months, 2 weeks, & 1 day

August 22nd

1948 | 46

18 days

4 months

45 years

page91

1 month

1952 | 47

31 years

6 months, 3 weeks, & 4 days

April 26th

16 days

December 7th

October

March 7th

Sara's by 3 days

page92

3 months, 2 weeks, & 2 days

return ?February 22nd

September 5th

1946 | 49

October 12th

August

Melanie's by 2 days

15 days

29 years

1 month

page93

3 months

19 days

s on Tom's by 4 days

35 years

August 6th

1954 | 42

August

6 months, 3 weeks, & 2 days

May 11th

March 17th

page94

November

:ket ?September 12th

17 days

July 26th

13 years

2 months

Tim's by 2 days

7 months, 2 weeks, & 4 days

1979 | 31

November 11th

page95

1972 | 33

?September 6th

May

27 years

Tim's by 4 days

August 6th

4 months, 1 week, & 3 days

10 days

January 11th

4 months

page96

February 9th

51 years

12 days

September 4th

6 months, 2 weeks, & 3 days

Sally's by 2 days

July 2nd

November

4 months

1964 | 48

page97

10 days

October 12th

1954 | 48

November 13th

11 months

August 26th

Jessica's by 5 days

May

23 years

8 months, and 3 days

page98

35 years

1955 | 48

9 months, 1 week, & 1 day

February 11th

June

Jason's by 5 days

2 months

5 days

November 7th

July 4th

page99

September

March 7th

4 months, and 4 days

6 days

44 years

January 6th

April 16th

Tom's by 4 days

6 months

1942 | 40

page100

10 days

October 12th

1954 | 48

November 13th

11 months

August 26th

Jessica's by 5 days

May

23 years

8 months, and 3 days

FINISH

Printed in Great Britain
by Amazon